Verse & Universe

Verse & Universe

POEMS ABOUT
SCIENCE AND MATHEMATICS

EDITED BY

KURT BROWN

MILKWEED EDITIONS

© 1998, Selection and arrangement by Kurt Brown
Each author holds copyright to his or her poem.
All rights reserved. Except for brief quotations in critical articles or reviews, no part of this book may be reproduced in any manner without prior written permission from the publisher: Milkweed Editions, 430 First Avenue North, Suite 400, Minneapolis, MN 55401
Distributed by Publishers Group West

Published 1998 by Milkweed Editions
Printed in the United States of America
Cover design by Adrian Morgan, Red Letter Design
Interior design by Will Powers
The text of this book is set in Charlotte.
98 99 00 01 02 5 4 3 2 1
First Edition

The epigraphs on p. xv are from Edward Abbey, *The Journey Home* (New York: E. P. Dutton, 1977), 87; and George Steiner, *In Bluebeard's Castle* (New Haven, N.J.: Yale University Press, 1971), 131–32.

Milkweed Editions is a not-for-profit publisher. We gratefully acknowledge support from Elmer L. and Eleanor J. Andersen Foundation; James Ford Bell Foundation; Dayton's, Mervyn's, and Target Stores by the Dayton Hudson Foundation; Doherty, Rumble and Butler; Dorsey and Whitney Foundation; General Mills Foundation; Honeywell Foundation; Hubbard Foundation; Jerome Foundation; McKnight Foundation; Andrew W. Mellon Foundation; Minnesota State Arts Board through an appropriation by the Minnesota State Legislature; Challenge and Creation and Presentation Programs of the National Endowment for the Arts; Norwest Foundation on behalf of Norwest Bank Minnesota, Norwest Investment Management and Trust, Lowry Hill, Norwest Investment Services, Inc.; Lawrence and Elizabeth Ann O'Shaughnessy Charitable Income Trust in honor of Lawrence M. O'Shaughnessy; Oswald Family Foundation; Piper Jaffray Companies, Inc.; Ritz Foundation on behalf of Mr. and Mrs. E. J. Phelps Jr.; John and Beverly Rollwagen Fund of the Minneapolis Foundation; St. Paul Companies, Inc.; Star Tribune/Cowles Media Foundation; James R. Thorpe Foundation; and generous individuals.

Library of Congress Cataloging-in-Publication Data

   Verse and universe : poems about science and mathematics / edited by Kurt Brown. — 1st ed.
      p. cm.
     ISBN 1-57131-407-5 (alk. paper)
     1. Science—Poetry. 2. Mathematics—Poetry.
     3. American poetry—20th century. I. Brown, Kurt.
     PS595.S348V47 1998
     811.008'0356—dc21   98-19340
                                          CIP

This book is printed on acid-free paper.

For Mathieu de Schutter

To all who encouraged me in this undertaking

Keith Allen Daniels for leading me to scientists who are also poets
M. L. Williams for his poetry and expert overview
Bruce Berger for collecting a number of these poems unbidden
Thomas Krampf for his passion and support
my wife, Laure-Anne Bosselaar, for living with primal chaos

and of course Emilie Buchwald and everyone at Milkweed Editions
who continue to sustain and support my editorial projects

Verse and Universe

Introduction

6. EARTH

7. ANIMAL

8. HUMAN

9. THEORY AND SPECULATION

Introduction

With two notable exceptions—Loren Eiseley (naturalist, anthropologist, paleontologist) and Roald Hoffmann (recipient of the Nobel Prize for chemistry in 1981)—the poets represented here are not scientists. The work they produce is not science, but art. Poems focusing on scientific themes—like any other poems—wind up as disquisitions on loneliness or chance, love, praise, hope, despair, or any number of other subjects from the timeless infinity of human experience. A poem's connection to science and mathematics is largely utilitarian: different fields of knowledge are explored for themes, images, metaphors, and language that might be used in the making of new and unique poems.

The poems in this book, then, reveal for the rest of us unexpected meanings in the work of scientists and mathematicians. I have chosen many poets whose work is saturated with knowledge of scientific theory and research, while others might be represented by a single poem not indicative of their work as a whole. What they make of such knowledge can be as surprising and wonderful as the initial scientific findings themselves. That is, finally, the real purpose of this anthology: to bring science and mathematics to us in a form we might begin to understand, and in which we might take some unusual delight; to record our psychological, emotional, and intellectual responses to facts and discoveries we might otherwise have no way of apprehending properly.

In the interest of focus I have chosen only American poets writing in the second half of this century, and I made a distinction, early on, between science and technology. By science, I mean the pure study of the universe and all it contains for the sake of knowledge and understanding alone, keeping in mind the Latin root of the word *scire*, to know. Technology, it seems to me, is really the application of scientific principles for practical, and economic, ends. And medicine, however crucial for human existence, is technology in action. The pure study of the universe might include, therefore, what we have traditionally termed the physical sciences—physics, astronomy, chemistry, geology, and so on—and the life sciences, which include biology, botany, zoology, and physiology, among others. A secondary purpose of this book is to stimulate interest in poetry and science alike, and to lead the reader a few intriguing steps in both directions.

Debates about the relationship between science and mathematics on one hand, and art on the other—the so-called schism that occurred, probably in the eighteenth century, leaving a wide crack down the center of western intellectual life—I leave to others with far more ability and knowledge. The subject is a huge one and has already generated libraries of complicated texts. There have always been people on both sides of this divide, however, who are uncomfortable with the situation as it stands. Perhaps the kind of imagination it takes to conceive of a radical and complicated new scientific theory, and prove it, is not so different from what is required to envision, compose and successfully execute a great poem. The human mind may not be as compartmentalized or fractured as we tend to believe. If science and art have anything in common it exists in the resources of the human brain and our ability to create something unforeseen and revolutionary out of our dreaming.

KURT BROWN
Cambridge, Massachusetts, 1997

Any good poet, in our age at least, must begin with the scientific view of the world; and any scientist worth listening to must be something of a poet, must possess the ability to communicate to the rest of us his sense of love and wonder at what his work discovers.

EDWARD ABBEY, The Journey Home

The notion that one can exercise a rational literacy in the latter part of the twentieth century without a knowledge of calculus, without some preliminary access to topology or algebraic analysis, will soon seem a bizarre archaism. These style and speech-forms from the grammar of number are already indispensible to many branches of modern logic, philosophy, linguistics, and psychology. They are the language of feeling where it is today most adventurous. As electronic data-processing and coding pervade more and more of the economics and social order of our lives, the mathematical illiterate will find himself cut off. A new hierarchy of menial service and stunted opportunity may develop among those whose resources continue to be purely verbal. There may be "word-helots."

GEORGE STEINER, In Bluebeard's Castle

Verse & Universe

1
Verse niverse

Long has creation been taken as that live tongue . . .

EMILY HIESTAND

DAVID IGNATOW

Poet to Physicist in His Laboratory

Come out and talk to me
for then I know
into what you are shaping.
Thinking is no more,
I read your thoughts for a symbol:
a movement towards an act.
I give up on thought
as I see your mind
leading into a mystery
deepening about you.
What are you trying to discover
beyond the zone of habit
and enforced convention?
There is the animus
that spends itself on images,
the most complex being
convention and habit.
You shall form patterns
of research and bind yourself
to laws within your knowledge,
and always conscious of your limitations
make settlement,
with patience to instruct you
as it always does
in your research: an arrangement
spanning an abyss of time,
and you will find yourself patient
when you are questioned.

Earth's Answer

Another night of Galileo arguing with William Blake—
the one with an angel in his tree, believing
"Where humans are not, nature is barren."
The other, *il saggiotore* and curious Venetian,
pointing politely to his optical tube:

If the gentleman would look out the window, at the moons

[the Moons of Ellipsis]

No more sleeping this night, so rising I struggle with bards.
One heard the furnace, Orc-rending an ocean,
all Beulah weeping. And one saw the revolution.

Long has creation been taken as that live tongue
telling in crumbling ores and recumbent folds,
in fugitive colors and the long clear combs of the sea.
Indifferent, the plenum yet sounds as siren
and provocateur on the drum of our whorlèd ears—
down dainty canals made by thunder and moan.

Yet loosed as we are from the eerie circuitry of ants,
we wander, and wandering weave a likening tissue.
Even Galileo's descendants, in the deep sweet dream
of objectivity weave, as once a physicist, dismissing metaphor
and all its errancy, said, by way of illustration,
"The planet is only a tennis ball, with a bit of fuzz for life."

I did not chortle, believe me, I did not mock. I sympathized.
Numberless, the natures of a world that keeps faith
and does the astronomer's will as well.
As first light comes, the mortar and pestle on my sill
grow flagrantly red in the sun, burning as the need to know.
The goods look ripe to be stolen, and I could use that red,
that unhurried crimsom-salmon surefire sanguine bloom.
Only lead us not, we pray, into petty thieving.

Madonnas Touched Up with a Goatee

Most ancient Metaphysics, (poor Metaphysics!)
All decked up in imitation jewelry.
We went for a stroll, arm in arm, smooching in public
Despite the difference in ages.

It's still the 19th century, she whispered.
We were in a knife-fighting neighborhood
Among some rundown relics of the Industrial Revolution.
Just a little further, she assured me,
In the back of a certain candy store only she knew about,
The customers were engrossed in the *Phenomenology of the Spirit*.

It's long past midnight, my dove, my angel!
We'd better be careful, I thought.
There were young hoods on street corners
With crosses and iron studs on their leather jackets.
They all looked like they'd read Darwin and that madman Pavlov,
And were about to ask us for a light.

The Poet Studies Physics

FOR GUY MURCHIE

As the milk bursts its electric skin,
spills over the rim and streams
to the floor in a series of varying
pear shapes and globes only a fast
camera sees, or at that peak in trajectory
when the hurled glass seems to pause,
burning our retinas with its existence
before it ceases to exist,
we think we have found it, apparent
luminosity, the wholly logical *now*,
that state Greek logicians worried like meat,
fumbling for some medial bone.

Between the beginning, the first step,
and infinite, breathing worlds,
these things gather together:

a number small as the average family;

the eye of a mountain quail;

a scale that will never balance,
its needle drifting endlessly
to nearer and farther extremes;

the center of the universe;

a boy's pocket, filled with stones;

our pencils attempting these ellipses
with elusive focal points—
coral polyp,
quasar,
treble clef,
rose.

Figures of Thought

To lay the logarithmic spiral on
Sea-shell and leaf alike, and see it fit,
To watch the same idea work itself out
In the fighter pilot's steepening, tightening turn
Onto his target, setting up the kill,
And in the flight of certain wall-eyed bugs
Who cannot see to fly straight into death
But have to cast their sidelong glance at it
And come but cranking to the candle's flame—

How secret that is, and how privileged
One feels to find the same necessity
Ciphered in forms diverse and otherwise
Without kinship—that is the beautiful
In Nature as in art, not obvious,
Not inaccessible, but just between.

It may diminish some our dry delight
To wonder if everything we are and do
Lies subject to some little law like that;
Hidden in nature, but not deeply so.

Computer Map of the Early Universe

We're made of stars. The scientific team
Flashes a blue and green computer chart
Of the universe across my TV screen
To prove its theory with a work of art:
Temperature shifts translated into waves
Of color, numbers hidden in smooth lines.
"At last we have a map of ancient Time"
One scientist says, lost in a rapt gaze.
I look at the bright model they've designed,
The Big Bang's fury frozen into laws,
Pleased to see it resembles a sonnet,
A little frame of images and rhyme
That tries to glitter brighter than its flaws
And trick the truth into its starry net.

Poems Overheard at a Conference on Relativity Theory

I.

It may be possible to quantize
gravity in the harmonic gauge
with ghost fields.

Einstein's equations do not hold,
and thus the theory differs
from that in the temporal gauge.

But if the quantum states
are chosen carefully, then we may find
scattering amplitudes

equal to the others corresponding
in the temporal gauge.
Not everybody sees

the quantum theory of gravity
with ghosts differs in content
from that in the temporal gauge.

The problem is, equations
involving infinity
must turn out meaningless,

so quantum states may not
be normalizable. We cannot form
inner products with such states.

But if we adiabatically
switch off the interaction,
the functional integrations

over g sub 0 sub mu,
as well as all the ghost fields,
yield unity. And hence,

the scattering amplitudes
must in the end be equal to the others
corresponding in the temporal gauge.

II.

How can a spatio-temporally extended
picture of matter evolving, be reconciled
with the broad indeterminism appropriate
to the concept of chance?

An essentially probabilistic physics
(as ours is commonly assumed to be)
rests on a logic of intersubjectivity
different from Bayesian.

Probability governs the causal order,
the latter in turn propagating the probable,
just as in thermodynamics, entropy governs
exchanges of energy.

Entropy's much like mislaid information;
information is carried as organized energy.
If we could see at a finer level, it might not
appear to increase so sharply.

Synthesized in Dirac's "bras" and "kets,"
the early Born-Jordan wavelike recipe
for handling quantum probabilities
was later dressed by Feynman

in manifestly relativistic form:
add partial and multiply the independent
amplitudes, not probabilities.
Consider wave intensity.

Definitely not involved in a poker game,
observers of two very distant events

know a symmetric binding exists between them
as a telegraph termed "the field."

This symmetry entails determination,
not determinism: acting in the past
and seeing in the future aren't forbidden,
only strongly repressed.

So chance is more than fact-like accident.
It is the law-like power that representation,
Janus of a final cause, employs
to turn its semblance into reality.

III.

How does light know how
        to take the shortest path?

Why are straight lines also
        the shortest lines?

Why is there any geometry
        at all?

IV

Holonomic fields
cover a wide class of material schemes,
particularly perfect fluids
and hence pure matter (dusts).

The current lines of holonomic fields
are geodesics of the Riemannian
manifold v, g bar:
g bar equals F squared g.

F is the index of the material field.
In the case of pure matter (dusts)

F equals one, and g bar equals g.
Thus absolute time's defined.

Within the usual hypotheses
of a universe U containing
a perfect, homogeneous, isotropic
fluid identified

by comobile coordinates, apply
Robertson and Walker's tensor;
then we may define t bar
as cosmological time.

This shows that in the case
where a gravitational field
interacts with a holonomic material
field, the light describes

the geodesics of U, g bar.
Thus the units of length and time
should be deduced from the tensor
g bar, not g alone.

We do not have, not yet,
a single equation of state
valid at every density
for a cosmological fluid.

Still, we may define three phases:
when density exceeds the nuclear;
when radiation predominates; and when
the fluid consists of dust.

Thus Big Bang is just an illusion,
because we are measuring past events
using our present time-scale.
Really, we should find another time-scale.

V.

General relativistic spacetime
geometry may be given
solely in terms of a threefold relation
between events: beta of A, B, C,
events at a freely falling particle.
B happens in between the A and C.
Our proof makes use of various results,
like Schild's that construct clocks
from freely falling particles and light rays.
We'd like to construct a clock that ticks
by purely synthetic means,
without supposing differentiable structure.

Consider Castagnino's clock: expand
the coordinate expressions for tick-events,
particles, and light rays into powers
of epsilon, and then work out
the linear and the quadratic terms.
For light rays and geodesic particles
quadratic terms must vanish.
It follows that g is a smooth, non-vanishing function,
and g is the constant function 1
for the geodesic case, where lamba becomes
a smooth non-vanishing function, identical
with t, and t is time.

Problem: because we need
an arbitrarily large number of ticks,
we have to prove that the clock won't explode.

VI.

Evidence that the universe expands
in strict accordance with the Big Bang theory.

1.
The age of the most ancient stars
corresponds to the age of the universe
obtained from the decay
of radioactive elements. The match is good,
especially when we introduce a cosmic
repulsion which in turn explains
why macrobubbles have been formed,
big nothings lodged inside our universe.

2.
The average barionic density
matches the average density (including
that of the hypothetical dark mass)
obtained from the free fall of our local group
of home stars, towards the cluster we call Virgo.

3.
The evolution of the galaxies
reveals their light was bluer once,
just when the first big stars were being formed.
Supernovae of the massive stars
exploded; red ones, smaller ones, remained.

The evolution of the universe
is now explained in detail,
up to and even including the genesis
of planets from the dust
of supernovae as they all exploded.

4.
Starquakes have been detected
in pulsars, as predicted.
And some in ours, equation or galaxy.

VII.

The labor of being at the source,
or rather, of being the source of time
that comes towards us in the shape
of world from the to-come,
endlessly repeating itself
without resembling itself:
this is the great Act.

The Person at the source of the arrival
of such persistent mystery must abscond,
or otherwise be merely
a being among beings in the world.
Hence that Person, source of ways and places,
doesn't abscond in space, that mere
fiction of the human mind.

It must abscond in time,
or better, behind time, that is, behind
the to-come, and the world as *parousia*,
always renewed by temporal surprises.
Thus we assume that even Miracle
remains a possibility, and bide.

Farder to Reache

Kepler was born in 1571. He knew about as much of the night sky and its mysteries as anyone alive in his time. We might say his skull *contained* the sky of the 16th and early 17th centuries, held it in place like a planetarium dome. Today we still haven't improved on his famous three Laws of Planetary Motion.

And yet the notion that the universe might be infinite—that there wasn't an outermost sphere of stars that bound it all in—terrified him, filled him with what he termed "secret, hidden horror . . . One finds oneself wandering in this immensity in which are denied limits and center."

This is, of course, the dread of free verse, that one might fall into Whitman and freefloat directionlessly forever. Whitman *calls* himself "a Kosmos," and in "Song of Myself" the vision is of a creation whose parts are "limitless" and "numberless"—these words and their kin are used with manic glee and with a great intentionality. This is poetry's announcement of the given of 20th-century astronomy: the universe is, so far as we know, unbounded.

But it isn't easy to walk through a day of fists and kisses, paychecks, diaperstains, tirejacks, and our buildingblock aspirations, with the mind fixed on infinity. Every year in beginning poetry classes hands startle up in protest of free verse, "it isn't *poetry*," which is metered and rhymed, and so is a kind of map of Kepler's universe.

John Donne's poems, for instance—he was born one year after Kepler. And he praises his lover by placing her at the center of an onion-ring sky: "so many spheres, but one heaven make," and "they are all concentric unto thee."

And yet as early as 1577—Kepler was only 6 years old—the British astronomer Thomas Digges undid the outer sphere, and published a vision of stars in endlessness: "Of which lightes celestiall, it is to bee thoughte that we onely behoulde sutch as are in the inferioure partes . . . even tyll our sighte being not able farder to reache or conceyve, the greatest part rest by reason of their wonderfull distance invisible unto us."

Perhaps infinity isn't discovered along a timeline of gathering progress, but by certain sensibility, no matter when it lives.

In that land of simultaneous sensibility, I think I could knock on Kepler's door and invite him out for some beers with Whitman. Really: he's flinging his cloak on now.

It's a foggy night as we sit around the verandah overlooking the lake. The sky is cloudy, and so are my two friends' faces—they don't know each other, are guarded, and rely on me to ease the conversation.

I do, though; or maybe it's the beer. It turns out we can shoot the shit all night, stein after stein, anecdote on anecdote, until the first light swarms over the water like thistledown on fire. Then the fog disappears—which is, of course, the day clearing its throat for speech.

2
Space

Looking up, we just keep falling . . .

ALISON HAWTHORNE DEMING

FREDERICK SEIDEL

The New Cosmology

Above the Third World, looking down on a fourth:
Life's aerial photograph of a new radio telescope
Discoloring an inch of mountainside in Chile,
A Martian invasion of dish receivers.
The tribes of Israel in their tents
Must have looked like this to God—
A naive stain of wildflowers on a hill,
A field of ear trumpets listening for Him,
Stuck listening to space like someone blind . . .

If there was a God.
There never is.
Almond-eyed shepherd warriors
Softly pluck their harps and stare off into space,
And close their eyes and dream.
In one tent, the Ark;
The chip of kryptonite.
They dream a recurring dream
About themselves as superpowers, and their origin.

Man is the only animal that dreams of outer space,
Epitome of life on earth,
The divine mammal which can dream
It is the chosen people of the universe
No more. But once you have got up high enough to look down,
Once you have got out far enough to look back,
The earth seems to magnify itself
In intensely sharp focus against the black,
Beautiful blind eye milky blue.

That we are alone, that we are not, are unimaginable.
We turn a page of *Life*,
Lying open in the grass,
To a pink earthworm slowly crossing the Milky Way

At nearly the speed of light—red-shifted protein!
The rest is unimaginable,
Like the silence before the universe.
The last nanosecond of silence twenty billion years ago
Before the big bang is endless.

DINAH BERLAND

All Together, Nothing Lost

It hit the news today: the telescopic evidence,
faint light from cosmic gas, traces of the stuff
that once held everything at once—my fingernail, this pen,
pendulum clock, the wicker chair in which I sit, my mother's
hairnets, the bird that once perched on her bun, Father's
movies of the Ohio River flood, the plane that crashed
in Dallas yesterday, unopened parachutes dangling
from the trees like streamers, the cameo that vanished
under the bed when I was ten, mountains
of bleached conch shells, women washing sheets
in the Ganges, every Brahma bull that ever
watched them, eyeballs, hoofs and tongues,
corned beef and cabbage, taffy apples, the braids
my grandfather cut from my head when I was
seven, the smell of his hand-rolled
cigars, Hemingway's lost suitcase, my friend Ruth's
new baby Annie, her prehensile toes, every cactus and
machete, funeral pyres, bonfires, my absent son,
surgeons in white coats, scalpels, stethoscopes, blunt
weapons, nuclear inventions, rivers, fly rods, your
testicles, my breasts, El Greco's horses and El Greco,
Galileo buried with one bony finger pointing at the stars,
the letters *aleph, beth, gimel, daleth*, cobbled streets
of Paris, craters on the moon, spaceships not invented yet
and cameras clicking pictures of that cosmic dust
colder than the pain of loss—proving that everything came
from the same infinitesimal seed
about the size, they say, of the dot at the end of this sentence.

Astronomer

Far far
Beyond the stargazer
The astronomer

Who does not try
To make the sky
His sky

But goes out of his mind
To find
Beyond.

Nightly he goes
Nightly he knows
Where no comfort is

And this
His comfort is
His irreducible peace.

Uncanny traveler
To leave himself how far
Behind.

CHRISTOPHER BUCKLEY

Star Journal

Astronomy is for the soul—
            the truth about what
                        and who we are
                                    and will be.
The universe grinding blithely away
                        and we, reflective grist, stellar pollen
cooling down enough to somewhere
                        finally shine—
                        a caucus of dust and acids blown
over the warped table of space,
                        arriving on the shirttails of comets to lap down
on tundra, settle on
            palmetto leaves, blinking above an isthmus white with sand . . .

*   *   *

And so unconsciously we take our breaths
                        into orbit about the solar apparatus
of the heart—
            star with its own fusion and collapse—each measure and molecule
voluble but
            unaccountable in a code
                        comprising even the weightless freight
of thought
            as we stand out each night exhaling
                        dim clouds from the ghosted
wingspan of our lungs . . .

*   *   *

We have built machines
            that can see light burning
                        from the lost beginning—
faint quasars, a printout just coming
                        through the hazed background buzz
after fifteen billion years.

*   *   *

From our vantage point in the outer precincts,
                              we tune in radio from the first
broadcast, big downbeat still on every network
                              and starry frequency
as we go for a spin through the galactic plasma,
                              a kind of Dyna-Flow along
the boulevards,
              oxbows and sluice gates of time ...

                    *   *   *

Telescopes *are* time machines—
                              lanes for recovered light
                                        bringing the past
up to speed,
              pulling down the crystal spheres
                                        and broken symmetries,
                                                  exposing
our surroundings, our irrepressible, elemental histories
                              with which we continue
to negotiate
              as if the wheel were firmly in our hands ...

                    *   *   *

Space itself is slipping away,
                    expanding,
                              but into what?
                                   Aristarchus of Samos, against
Ptolemy and the popular astrophysics, deduced
                              that earth was a planet, that stars were very far
away indeed!
              A little over 2,000 years
                              and this information was confirmed.
                              Still, there is the black
frame of space,
              stars untrue in our parallax view—their bent scintillations

                              so many curve balls
breaking at the last instant over the outside corner
                              of the plate—
                    and so our doubt about everything
published above us in the dark—
                    and then the blank and sweeping margins of the east
each dawn
            after we've again tried to decipher the shorthand in the night.

                              *   *   *

Sitting up at dawn, starlings appear
                    across the lawn like black holes in the mist-bright sheen.
            Birds congregate, begin a cappella—cavatinas and recitatives—
without the least
                introspection, time-management or stress,
                                neither do they sew . . .
A steady disregard of the attrition in the air,
                        the ambiguous blue going of the world—
something like a rose-colored nebula
                    boiling in their breasts, moving them
to praise no matter the implications,
                    the copyright of the cold.

                              *   *   *

The lawn sprinklers whirl out their silver
                        and unerring loops . . .
                                    Gravity
keeps us here,
            the weak force and the strong force,
                            the invisible and
the dissembled something in the unified field—
                        even as light is fused
and driven through charged tines of air,
                        torching the tree, black Y against
the mustard sky, wringing out the horizon,

ash of its arms extended—funnel cloud
taking farm house and Ford Galaxy sedan
                                                    up the violet ascension of the sky
against that gravity and half the Midwest
                              on the TV A.M. news, particles accelerated,
snowy dots of channels flipped through.
                                        Out the window, the glitter in the night
river washed away, discord of black
                              sand rolling over some last bright bones—
wing bones, let's say,
                    holding it all up
                              about us as we reel outward, carrying
our blue and parochial atmosphere with us,
                                        our little argument advanced
against all the blind stuff of space,
                              the dark matter now ninety per cent of everything,
denser than anthracite with time,
                              dead energy so massed it will never shine,
nor harbor one mote of mica,
                    one iced diamond-fleck
                                        not inked and unknowable.
Only its gravitational arcs, its fingerprints hold
                              the pearl-like and whirling
Milky Way in thrall, keep the arms swirled
                                        brilliantly together, rotating in sync
with the yolky center, edges bright
                              with the hum and singing of atoms swimming
outward, burning away
                    somewhere nothing ends.

ALISON HAWTHORNE DEMING

Mt. Lemmon, Steward Observatory, 1990

What it takes to dazzle us, masters of dazzle,
all of us here together at the top of the world,
is a night without neon or mercury lamps.
Black sheen flowing above,
the stars, unnamed and disorderly—
diamonds, a ruby or sapphire,
scattered and made
more precious for being cut
from whatever strand
once held them together.
The universe is emptiness and dust,
occasional collisions, collapsing zones of gas,
electrical bursts, and us.

Here is the 60-inch scope where
we struggle to see one pinpoint of light,
each singularity with its timid twinkle
become a city of stars, that trapezoidal
grouping at the end of Orion's sword,
a cloudy nursery spawning
galactic stuff, lit but not illuminated
by a glassy hot blue star. What is it to see?
A mechanism wired in the brain
that leads to wonder. What is it
to wonder but to say
what we've seen and, having said it,
need to see farther.

Here are the globulars and spirals,
the dumbbell, ring, and crab—particles
swept like water in a drain, shapes
mapping the torque that shapes them,
tension of matter, micro- and
macro-scopic, orbiting, electron

and planet straining at apogee
like a husky on the leash.
Here is Pegasus, the Great Square—
call it the Baseball Diamond, a story
we can see, one we can use
to find our way back. A scientist
can say *NGC 5194/5* to another
and the other says *Ahhh,*
picturing the massive whirlpool, its
small companion galaxy eddying by its side.

Call it the Nipple with a nearby Mole,
call it the Chief Executive Officer
walking his Spitz. Describing *is* imagining—
knowing, not knowing but
having the language
to convey, to *be* the water carrier,
Aquarius, to quench another.
I saw it with my own eyes.
Seeing is believing.
That paloverde tree is green.
On earth as it is in heaven.
But the sky is not blue
and the stars are not a drifting dome,
merely coordinates plotted on
the immensity inside—
the Eternity we walk in when we dream.

Still the universe (the way we see it)
is more real than Heraclitus,
who said the stars were solid bowls
filled with fire, fire which feeds
on the ocean's watery breath.
Why not, since water is consumed
by fire, imagine it as food?
Why not think the brain's

favorite food is seeing?
We still don't know what light is.
Where matter comes from. How the dust
became fire. Why our fire must
turn to dust. And all we have to go on
(refining the instrument) is our selves—
the skin at the tips of our fingers.

All we have to go on is ignorance—
to pay attention to what we've missed.
tides? Amorph—
one scientist's notation in
The Atlas of Galaxies
beneath a shapeless smudge.
They have to take it seriously, everything
they see, trying to invent
a way to pass it on. In this
they are poets as much as
the visitor who says,
Ohhh, a shooting star,
after she's been told
nothing is burning, nothing shooting,
merely molecules of sky jumping
as dust from beyond whizzes by.
Here is the world's biggest mirror—

a million dollars to cast
the glass in hexagonal molds,
to spin the gleaming saucer
parabolic, then a computer
to cool it cell by cell—
six weeks of that and then another
million, two years to polish
the surface to digital perfection.
Here are those gods and goddesses
seen for what they are—battered rock

and frigid gas, sulfur boiling out
into murderous air—
all of us here together
watching from our blue oasis,
whirling in a frozen fading night
where there is not enough
matter to explain why any of it
is here.

Consider the moon. A fault
visible tonight near the terminator
looks like a crease in fresh plaster.
Sea of Rains, Ocean of Storms.
But it has never been moist,
never felt dew or rivers.
Marsh of Sleep, Sea of Ingenuity—
a map of our misunderstanding.
The wonder is we still can see
the way it pours liquid pearl
over the earth's dark waters
after we know its windless surface,
that implacable dust the moon travelers said
smelled like cap guns, is cratered
with a wire-braced flag, two lunar jeeps,
and footprints no weather will arrive to erase.

Here is the observatory at 1 A.M.,
white domes humming on the mountain top
like brains, antennae feeling
(a mechanism wired) their way
into the wilderness. They won't explain
a thing about the wealth
of blackberries in Labrador,
or the sleep of velvet bats
hanging in the eaves drugged by the sun.
They won't fix history or touch the places

inside we can't get close to.
Looking up, we just keep falling.
Here are the owls who navigate
in darkness, here the scattered prey.

CHRISTOPHER BUCKLEY

Isotropic

after the launching of the Hubble Space Telescope, April 25, 1990

Looked at in different directions,
the universe shows no significant
difference in its general appearance—
no blue shifts, nothing coming our way,
no change imminent; everything's red-shifted
and rotating outward, bright arm over arm
in the same expanding sea . . .

It's as if we've been standing
at the bottom of a pool, looking up
at the rippling colors and flights of birds,
the way we've had to chart and ponder
heavenly bodies beaming down to us
through stardust and patinas of our air.

Now a new observatory runs laps beyond
our atmosphere, copestone on that breathless ledge
of black—its floating beryllium eye
fixed on the unedited ticker-tape of light,
those naked lines exponentially deconstructing
in their own non stop play back of the past,
their medium the only message
about a point in time beyond any point
in time and that undoing that set things
spinning on the logarithm of the dark.

And though the new thinking sees it all
without the chaotic and misleading sprawl
of motes that's underwritten our reasoning
for so long and saved us from considering
a serious connection to design, some cataract
across the lens, it appears, will keep
this finally from us for yet a little while.

But even when the unfiltered news comes through,
is it likely we'll undergo a sea change,
so to speak, and find a bright new continent
at the heart of it instead of the one
we've been sailing for all along?

When I look up to the plaster and ceiling beams,
water-damaged from another season's rains,
I see amber ellipses and tea-colored swirls,
which, drifting toward the window and the wall,
look like dried roses or, equally, like nebulae
with their dense palm-print and smudge of suns.

Yet birds still slipstream on their magnetic,
star-gazed routes, and still the prevailing winds
pause a little and allow that cider scent of autumn
to loiter on the afternoon—the high western sky
reading left to right as always, and the blue
tree dahlias corresponding—
                          then the horizon
spills out like a glass of light and dust, the violet
overtones finely invisible as our breath
as we sit smiling among the fallen leaves,

collars turned up around our necks as we stare
inefficiently toward our old constabulary of stars,
that same light we've seen all along,
light which will one day rise
through our shoulder blades and arms
and set us blindly off, more white and weightless
than the air we leave behind.

CHARLES SIMIC

Many Zeros

The teacher rises voiceless before a class
Of pale, tight-lipped children.
The blackboard behind him as black as the sky
Light-years from the earth.

It's the silence the teacher loves,
The taste of the infinite in it.
The stars like teeth marks on children's pencils.
Listen to it, he says happily.

Achieving Perspective

Straight up away from this road,
Away from the fitted particles of frost
Coating the hull of each chick pea,
And the stiff archer bug making its way
In the morning dark, toe hair by toe hair,
Up the stem of the trillium,
Straight up through the sky above this road right now,
The galaxies of the Cygnus A cluster
Are colliding with each other in a massive swarm
Of interpenetrating and exploding catastrophes.
I try to remember that.

And even in the gold and purple pretense
Of evening, I make myself remember
That it would take 40,000 years full of gathering
Into leaf and dropping, full of pulp splitting
And the hard wrinkling of seed, of the rising up
Of wood fibers and the disintegration of forests,
Of this lake disappearing completely in the bodies
Of toad slush and duckweed rock,
40,000 years and the fastest thing we own,
To reach the one star nearest to us.

And when you speak to me like this,
I try to remember that the wood and cement walls
Of this room are being swept away now,
Molecule by molecule, in a slow and steady wind,
And nothing at all separates our bodies
From the vast emptiness expanding, and I know
We are sitting in our chairs
Discoursing in the middle of the blackness of space.
And when you look at me
I try to recall that at this moment

Somewhere millions of miles beyond the dimness
Of the sun, the comet Biela, speeding
In its rocks and ices, is just beginning to enter
The widest arc of its elliptical turn.

A. R. AMMONS

Cascadilla Falls

I went down by Cascadilla
Falls this
evening, the
stream below the falls,
and picked up a
handsized stone
kidney-shaped, testicular, and

thought all its motions into it,
the 800 mph earth spin,
the 190-million-mile yearly
displacement around the sun,
the overriding
grand
haul

of the galaxy with the 30,000
mph of where
the sun's going:
thought all the interweaving
motions
into myself: dropped

the stone to dead rest:
the stream from other motions
broke
rushing over it:
shelterless,
I turned

to the sky and stood still:
oh
I do
not know where I am going
that I can live my life
by this single creek.

On Learning on the Clearest Night Only 6000 Stars Are Visible to the Naked Eye

If seeing only 6000 stars with the naked eye
       awestrucks us to topple
            in drunken ecstasy
Or piss looking up in devout praise of being,
What would happen if we could truly perceive,
       comprehend and experience
           the zillions
       of stars galaxies universes
            pastpresentfuture?

And if, as scientists agree, we only use
       10% of our brain's potential,
Then the astonishment we sense
       is only 10% of the astonishment
          we could sense,
And so it would seem that what seems
       like dots of light twinkling
          in pretty patterns
     moving across the black
          is really enough to shatter us
     like goblets when the soprano
          hits the highest note.

And if the 10% of the brainpower we do use
       is ignorant of 99.9% of the totality
          of the Universe,
     perhaps a li'l vino in our goblet
          ain't a bad idea—
Perhaps a flask of wine
       in deep wilderness night
          is more powerful
     than the largest telescope.

Good Heavens

I

The common garden snail can't watch
the heavens and enumerate—600 young
stars in Perseus, one more hour
until full moon. It can't make lists—
pinwheel of Andromeda, comet fireball
of Tempel-Tuttle. It has never called
its slither the soft finger of night
nor its wound shell a frozen
galactic spin. Yet its boneless,
thumb-sized head is filled and totally
deaf with exactly the same tone
and timbre as the sky.

II

Winter Midnight

It seemed I was looking into the face
of a vendor, skin so dark
I couldn't focus at first,
the stark structure of his skull
tighter, blacker even than his eyes.
It was a vendor with his wares—glass
bulbs and seeds, silver goats, loops
and strings of copper, brass-cathedral
charms, polished couples on sticks
copulating, twisted bracelets
and rings—spread like a market
of stars on the blanket at his knees.
I thought I saw borders, ways
and measures in his onyx face.
A shifty hawker, a familiar swindler,
it was an old, skinny vendor on folded

knees, kneeling purple bones, a skeleton
of vestments, a posture of spirals
and stocks hovering above and below
his spread of sockets and hoops,
reaching, rocking, merchandising
at my elbow: *Kum, laydee, bye,*
kum by mine.

III

To imagine stars and flaming
dust wheeling inside the gut
of a blind, transparent fish
swimming out-of-sight in the black
waters of a cave a thousand years ago
is to suggest that the perfect
mystery of time, motion and light
remains perfect.

IV

Good—because the heavy burnings
and fumings of evolving
star clusters and extragalactic
cacophonies—because the flaming
Cygnus Loop, still whipping
and spewing sixty thousand years
after its explosion—because
the churning, disgorging womb
of the Great Nebula and the rushing
oblivions left from the collapse
of protostars—because suffocating
caverns of pulling, sucking gases
and pursuing, encircling ropes
of nuclear bombardments—
because erupting cauldrons

of double stars and multiple
stars flinging outward great
spires and towers of searing
poisons—because all of these
for this long have stayed
far, *far* away from our place.

CHRISTOPHER BUCKLEY

Speculation in Dark Air

Twilight was a short burn before the blue
bruise a day wears into—autumn ending,
tossing its black trees low against the sky,
the shoulders of the air slumped a bit, gone
ochre at the dim earth's blunted edge . . .

And this week the first fusilade of snow
flakes blowing in, all at once, the way stars
ambush this backdrop, this blank calyx,
and, apparitional, burst through the deep
azures to blink on before that absolute

rising of the night. But tonight the stars
sit out, neglected, benign, softly whirling
we know now, at the heart of nothing
so unknowable as we once thought—these
bright spinning islands no longer endless

in the stream, for we've finally tracked down
the limits of the envelope—the vast immeasurable
squared off, the universe now knotted somewhere
like the end of a long black balloon. But for all
our intents and purposes there's the infinite

latitude and vacancy of the dark, which is still
expanding, and billions of light-years are free
to unravel before it runs out. Yet everything
is more finite than before, as our best guesses go
mystically where this nothing ends, the other side

of all there is: and if space is curved, then curved
on what? Not even the proverbial thin air . . .
Big Bang, Unified Field Theory, these attractive
reasonings collapse everything back to that first
clapping of the cosmic hand, but come up short

against this new unbounded breathlessness,
or some immaterial wall that stops the last rondo
of our stars. This entire effect may be its own
cause. Even so, old questions have their weight—
What's beyond the vortex of our days? What stuff

if not the quick stuff we're made of? Whatever
is left of innocence must be ours, as we peek out
beneath the clouds, self-consciously arranging
the sky to explain each brilliance amid our sense
of loss—we would have the stars resemble us,

like the Japanese who send lanterns out to sea
to guide the souls . . . Or like, on one of the world's
highest lakes, the fishermen of Patzcuaro, Mexico,
who in their thin canoes skim the glassy surface
for the star-white and almost transparent fish

and, holding out cloud-like butterfly nets fully
in their arms, dip to the water as clouds pass by,
almost as if they were fishing only for those
quiet clouds. Perhaps they believe their hearts fill
with clouds or that at last they'll become clouds

and lift above it all, tied loosely to the slow
movement of this life and so not lost forever
to the world? They're content in what they know
and have no long-range fears beyond the sky.
Yet how much of this is sleight of hand, lost

in mirrors, the shifting opacities of the mind?
The mean distance of M 31 is 2.2 million light-years;
in the 30's it was 750,000—an easy oversight, given
our atmosphere's jaded scrim, the interstellar rain
of dusts. Each half century, facts change, as if physics

were just a matter of style; but by the time
we could ever tell of this star's death, of its im-
plosion to light-soaking cinders, we'd have fanned

out in our solar winds, countless among the black,
amoebic tides. Even now it could be burnt-out,

and what we have arriving is an unsourced drive
of light, the window dressing of the past in sus-
pended present tense? Everything being relative,
galaxies grow tired before our eyes, weary finally
in their floss and chorus. And though there's nowhere

else for us but in the rucksack of our flesh, though
we stare boldly to Andromeda or the Corona Borealis,
our breath sends up its small white flags, ultimately
surrendering our airy conceits, as we stand on this side
of the dark, shivering like the grass or like the stars.

PATTIANN ROGERS

Life in an Expanding Universe

It's not only all those cosmic
pinwheels with their charging solar
luminosities, the way they spin around
like the paper kind tacked to a tree trunk,
the way they expel matter and light
like fields of dandelions throwing off
waves of summer sparks in the wind,
the way they speed outward,
receding, creating new distances
simply by soaring into them.

But it's also how the noisy
crow enlarges the territory
above the landscape at dawn, making
new multiple canyon spires in the sky
by the sharp towers and ledges
of its calling; and how the bighorn
expand the alpine meadows by repeating
inside their watching eyes every foil
of columbine and bell rue, all
the stretches of sedges, the candescences
of jagged slopes and crevices existing there.

And though there isn't a method
to measure it yet, by finding
a golden-banded skipper on a buttonbush,
by seeing a blue whiptail streak
through desert scrub, by looking up
one night and imagining the fleeing
motions of the stars themselves, I know
my presence must swell one flutter-width
wider, accelerate one lizard-slip farther,
descend many stellar-fathoms deeper
than it ever was before.

The God of Galaxies

The god of galaxies has more to govern
Than the first men imagined, when one mountain
Trumpeted his anger, and one rainbow,
Red in the east, restored them to his love.
One earth it was, with big and lesser torches,
And stars by night for candles. And he spoke
To single persons, sitting in their tents.

Now streams of worlds, now powdery great whirlwinds
Of universes far enough away
To seem but fog-wisps in a bank of night
So measureless the mind can sicken, trying—
Now seas of darkness, shoreless, on and on
Encircled by themselves, yet washing farther
Than the last triple sun, revolving, shows.

The god of galaxies—how shall we praise him?
For so we must, or wither. Yet what word
Of words? And where to send it, on which night
Of winter stars, of summer, or by autumn
In the first evening of the Pleiades?
The god of galaxies, of burning gases,
May have forgotten Leo and the Bull.

But God remembers, and is everywhere.
He even is the void, where nothing shines.
He is the absence of his own reflection
In the deep gulf; he is the dusky cinder
Of pure fire in its prime; he is the place
Prepared for hugest planets: black idea,
Brooding between fierce poles he keeps apart.

Those altitudes and oceans, though, with islands
Drifting, blown immense as by a wind,
And yet no wind; and not one blazing coast

Where thought could live, could listen—oh, what word
Of words? Let us consider it in terror,
And say it without voice. Praise universes
Numberless. Praise all of them. Praise Him.

Heat Death

> . . . *the universe might eventually reach a temperature*
> *equilibrium in which . . . useful energy sources no longer*
> *exist to support life or even motion.*
> New Grolier Multimedia Encyclopedia

The stars will give up fusing hydrogen, spewing
helium into space. The clouds of dust six trillion
miles long in which people see plesiosaurs

or Jesus' face will stop condensing into stars.
The temperature in Mauna Kea and at Nome
will be the same. The temperature of a boy's

lips and a girl's breast will be the same.
The temperature of a song sparrow will be the same
as the temperature of the fog that made it puff

its feathers, trilling in my lemon tree.
Its small brown beak—bug-catching pliers—
will open no more. Heat death will come, of course,

long after the last glacier has vaporized,
the last boy and girl and song sparrow melted
into molecules. But I can't comprehend

a static soup of matter stretching endlessly.
To think of heat death, I must use human terms:
the edges of my curtains not glowing at dawn;

Miss Carol, my cat, not moaning to call hissing
Toms to my back yard; my arms, which ache
to pull you close, frozen forever at my sides.

3

Time

Where the simplest words like "in the beginning" explode . . .

REG SANER

Moment

Now, starflake frozen on the windowpane
All of a winter night, the open hearth
Blazing beyond Andromeda, the sea-
Anemone and the downwind seed, O moment
Hastening, halting in a clockwise dust,
The time in all the hospitals is now,
Under the arc-lights where the sentry walks
His lonely wall it never moves from now,
The crying in the cell is also now,
And now is quiet in the tomb as now
Explodes inside the sun, and it is now
In the saddle of space, where argosies of dust
Sail outward blazing, and the mind of God,
The flash across the gap of being, thinks
In the instant absence of forever: now.

Time and the Hour

The convulsive incision   tore light

from matter, image   from similitude, black vowels

croaked and flew   from the four-lettered name of God.

In diffuse nebulae,   non-luminous metals shined

in their planets.   The thirty intentions of the shadows

condensed below a brightness   the multitude

of species emitted, and Ras Algethi   glared in Hercules.

So the light came   to contain numbers

and the first   was intoxication

and Giotto was intoxicated   painting Scrovegni,

1306.   Out in the fields—wheat,

cockleburs, jimson—   a farmer stood up his hoe

and when that hoe was standing   on its own shadow,

he knew, and he was certain   that he knew.

PATTIANN ROGERS

The Definition of Time

In the same moment
That Kioka's great-great-grandfather died,
11,000 particles of frost dissolved into dew
On the blades of the woodrush,
And three water lily leaf beetles paused
Anticipating light making movements
Of their bodies in the weeds.

And in that same moment an earthworm
Swallowed a single red spore down its slimmest
Vein, and the chimney crayfish shoveled a whisker farther
Through slick pond-bottom silt, and one slow
Slice of aster separated its purple segment
From the bud.

Simultaneously the mossy granite along the ridge shifted
Two grains on its five-mile fault, and the hooves
Of ewe and pony, damp in the low-field fog,
Shook with that shift. The early hawk on the post
Blinked a drop of mist from its eye, and the black tern
With a cry flew straight up, remembering the marsh
By scent alone over the sandy hills.

And in that instant the field, carried
Without consent through the dark, held
Its sedges steady for the first turn
Into the full orange sun, and each tense sliver
Of pine on the mountains far to the east
Shone hot already in a white noon,
And in the dark night-sea far behind the field and forest,
The head of a single shark sperm pierced
An ovum and became blood.

The twelfth ring of the tallest redwood
Hardened its circle, and the first lick of the hatching

Goatweed butterfly was made tongue. And Kioka
And his ancestors call the infinite and continuous
Record they make of this moment, "The Book
Of the Beginning and the Chronicle of the End."

The Redshifting Web

1

The dragons on the back of a circular bronze mirror
swirl without end. I sit and am an absorbing form:
I absorb the outline of a snowy owl on a branch,
the rigor mortis in a hand. I absorb the crunching sounds
when you walk across a glacial lake with aquamarine
ice heaved up here and there twenty feet high.
I absorb the moment a jeweler pours molten gold
into a cuttlefish mold and it begins to smoke.
I absorb the weight of a pause when it tilts
the conversation in a room. I absorb the moments
he sleeps holding her right breast in his left hand
and know it resembles glassy waves in a harbor
in descending spring light. Is the mind a mirror?
I see pig carcasses piled up from the floor
on a boat docked at Wanxian and the cook
who smokes inadvertently drops ashes into soup.
I absorb the stench of burning cuttlefish bone,
and as moments coalesce see to travel far is to return.

2

A cochineal picker goes blind;

Mao, swimming across the Yangtze River,
was buoyed by underwater frogmen;

in the nursing home,
she yelled, "Everyone here has Alzheimer's!"

it blistered his mouth;

they thought the tape of *erhu* solos was a series of spy messages;

finding a bag of piki pushpinned to the door;

shapes of saguaros by starlight;

a yogi tries on cowboy boots at a flea market;

a peregrine falcon
shears off a wing;

her niece went through the house and took what she wanted;

"The sooner the better";

like a blindman grinding the bones of a snow leopard;

she knew you had come to cut her hair;

suffering: this and that:
iron 26, gold 79;

they dared him to stare at the annular eclipse;

the yellow pupils of a saw-whet owl.

3

The gold shimmer at the beginning of summer
dissolves in a day. A fly mistakes a
gold spider, the size of a pinhead, at the center
of a glistening web. A morning mushroom
knows nothing of twilight and dawn?
Instead of developing a navy, Ci Xi
ordered architects to construct a two story
marble boat that floats on a lotus-covered lake.
Mistake a death cap for Caesar's amanita
and in hours a hepatic hole opens into the sky.
To avoid yelling at his pregnant wife,
a neighbor installs a boxing bag in a storeroom;
he periodically goes in, punches, punches,
reappears and smiles. A hummingbird moth
hovers and hovers at a woman wearing a
cochineal-dyed flowery dress. Liu Hansheng

collects hypodermic needles, washes them
under a hand pump, dries them in sunlight,
seals them in Red Cross plastic bags,
resells them as sterilized new ones to hospitals.

4

Absorb a corpse-like silence and be a brass
cone at the end of a string beginning
to mark the x of stillness. You may puzzle
as to why a meson beam oscillates, or why
galaxies appear to be simultaneously redshifting
in all directions, but do you stop to sense
death pulling and pulling from the center
of the earth to the end of the string?
A mother screams at her son, "You're so stupid,"
but the motion of this anger is a circle.
A teen was going to attend a demonstration,
but his parents, worried about tear gas,
persuaded him to stay home: he was bludgeoned
to death that afternoon by a burglar.
I awake dizzy with a searing headache
thinking what nightmare did I have
that I cannot remember only to discover
the slumlord dusted the floor with roach powder.

5

Moored off Qingdao, before sunrise,
the pilot of a tanker is selling dismantled bicycles.
Once, a watchmaker coated numbers on the dial

with radioactive paint and periodically
straightened the tip of the brush in his mouth.
Our son sights the North Star through a straw

taped to a protractor so that a bolt
dangling from a string marks the latitude.
I remember when he said his first word, "Clock";

his 6:02 is not mine, nor is your 7:03 his.
We visit Aurelia in the nursing home and find
she is sleeping curled in a fetal position.

A chain-smoking acupuncturist burps, curses;
a teen dips his head in paint thinner.
We think, had I *this* then that would,

but subjunctive form is surge and ache.
Yellow tips of chamisa are flaring open.
I drop a jar of mustard, and it shatters in a wave.

6

The smell of roasted chili;

descending into the epilimnion;

the shape of a datura leaf;

a bank robber superglued his fingertips;

in the lake,
ocean-seal absorption;

a moray snaps up a scorpion fish;

he had to mistake and mistake;

burned popcorn;

he lifted the fly agaric off of blue paper
and saw a white galaxy;

sitting in a cold sweat;

a child drinking Coke out of a formula bottle
has all her teeth capped in gold;

chrysanthemum-shaped fireworks exploding over the water;

red piki passed down a ladder;

laughter;

as a lobster mold transforms a russula into a delicacy;

replicating an Anasazi
yucca fiber and turkey-feather blanket.

7

He looks at a series of mirrors: Warring States,
Western Han, Eastern Han, Tang, Song,
and notices bits of irregular red corrosion

on the Warring States mirror. On the back,
three dragons swirl in mist and April air.
After sixteen years that first kiss

still has a flaring tail. He looks at the TLV
pattern on the back of the Han mirror:
the mind has diamond points east, south, west, north.

He grimaces and pulls up a pile of potatoes,
notices snow clouds coming in from the west.
She places a sunflower head on the northwest

corner of the fence. He looks at the back
of the Tang mirror: the lion and the grape
pattern is so wrought he turns, watches her

pick eggplant, senses the underlying
twist of pleasure and surprise that
in mind they flow and respond endlessly.

8

I find a rufous hummingbird on the floor
of a greenhouse, sense a redshifting

along the radial string of a web.
You may draw a cloud pattern in cement
setting in a patio, or wake to
sparkling ferns melting on a windowpane.
The struck, plucked, bowed, blown
sounds of the world come and go.
As first light enters a telescope
and one sees light of a star when the star
has vanished, I see a finch at a feeder,
beans germinating in darkness;
a man with a pole pulls yarn out
of an indigo vat, twists and untwists it;
I hear a shout as a child finds *Boletus*
barrowsii under ponderosa pine;
I see you wearing an onyx and gold pin.
In curved space, is a line a circle?

9

Pausing in the motion of a stroke,
two right hands
grasping a brush;

    staring through a skylight
    at a lunar eclipse;

a great blue heron,
wings flapping,
landing on the rail of a float house;

    near and far:
    a continuous warp;

a neighbor wants to tear down this fence;
a workman covets it
for a *trastero*;

raccoons on the rooftop
eating apricots;

the character *xuan*—
dark, dyed—
pinned to a wall above a computer;

lovers making
a room glow;

weaving on a vertical loom:
sound of a comb,
baleen;

hiding a world in a world:
1054, a supernova.

Time

I have a friend whose hair is like time: dark
deranged coils lit by a lamp
when she bends back her head to laugh. A unique event,
such as the crucifixion of Christ, was not
subject to repetition, thought St. Augustine, and therefore
time is linear. Does the universe
have an end, a beginning? Yes, the former the door
through which she departs, the latter
the door by which she returns,
and in between there is no rest from wanting her.

Time—each moment of which a hair on a child's nape.
Time—the chain between the churning tractor and the stump.
Time—her gown tossed like a continent at the Creation.
Newton, an absolutist, thought time a container
in which the universe exists—nonending, nonbeginning.
Time—enamored, forgiven by dust,
and capable of calling a single blade of grass an oasis.
Time—of swivel, small streams, plinth, stanchions.
And then Kant says no, time does not apply
to the universe, only to the way we think about time.

Time—the spot where the violin touches the maestro's cheek.
Time—an endless range of cumulonimbus.
Time—Good Monarch of the deepest blue inevitable.
The relativists (with whom the absolutists,
as usual, disagree) argue that concepts of past,
present, and future are mind-dependent, i.e.,
would time exist without conscious beings?
O Ultimate Abstract, is there time
in time, is there rest, in time,
from wanting her?

Tomorrow Is a Difficult Idea

I'm courting the future, making an effort to love it more.
This doesn't come easy.
The wooly bear caterpillars are ambiguous about the weather,
and astronomy can't tell us if the sky will fall.
Tomorrow is a difficult idea. I don't want anything around here
to be gone.

It won't take long to change everything: all the leaves; all
the sidewalks flowing past the gardens in the circles of your
    sunglasses.
Since that morning you first asked me,
"Are you interested in fortunes?" you've earned your reputation
as a happy man, whose curiosity about disasters
is purely novelistic, who likes the threat of losing
what he loves to win: everything. Who rarely has enough.
I can't stand an unknown world. Does probability control us?
How long will we last?
When I'm most certain you will leave me, I'm not frightened of the
        future,
but the past, its disasters so ignoble no one said "The Will of God."
You tell me, "A book makes up its ending and surprises you."

Do you have to be so sure?
When the cards tell me this won't be the day you leave,
you comment, "Life doesn't work that way."
You're also unaware I tell myself that I can always die,
as if it were just another option, one I'd tried before.

Einstein's God had to make this world,
its future unfolding with constrained randomness.
So the digressions in our narratives are choices
we have little choice about. As for my heroine,
she's a comic figure trying to look tragic
who grows up in three days,
whose hero shouts warnings from *Malachi* in bed.
Counting the time we'll have spent getting lost,

and if I don't say, "Leave me"
out of fear you'll leave me,
what portion of my story will be yours?

When you first went out to seek your fortune, your future,
you saw it pre-figured everywhere: in oil puddles, animal tracks.
Later, you'd wait decades for a favor from the God of numbers.
One afternoon, thirty-five years from now, while admiring
your accumulated hours and riches, your amazing choices and
        advantages,
you'll sense you are not destined to play poker that night.
    You'll see a tiny leak in fate to rush through
like a victor who meets other victors halfway and embraces them.
Leaning with God out of every window,
you'll see the whole game laid out, transparent,
all the action played out all at once.
    Maybe you'll reflect upon the fate of the sad waitress
or of the baby whose vocation as a bag lady
gypsies have foretold.
Or of this woman whom you've left.
    Is there room ahead for her?
You'd say, "There are no ultimate predictions,
but so far, literature and heaven are both open."

As for the basic questions about the future;
Will ballroom dancing spins come back in style?
Is there just one ending? May I press you, first,
between my thighs in a continuous birth of days and nights?
Then I'll have no choice but to die happy.
    Or to ask for something definite. A future.
A past. To know what we have.

ALANE ROLLINGS

About Time

I've been acting like today was something special.
At dawn, bums come to the street. At 8:00, while cleaning women
are arriving at the offices, you catch a train. (They say
there's no such thing as time; it's just imaginary.)

At 9:00, workers take their imaginations into offices; life can afford to
be wasteful. Think of Van Gogh, with wind in his beard while the sun
baked his brain. (Oh, to be a master of nature, solve the mysteries
of art, expectancy, science, sadness.)

I've met every train since 6:00. Recognizable, like life, by unlikelihood,
it's just like you to be nowhere. I hum some Schubert, stop. Life stopped
at 6 o'clock. Time's the problem. Sunday's perfect and complete, a finished
thing. It's Monday. With Van Gogh's faceless clock before me, I meet a train.
A boy waves from a train that takes him from Chicago. I run alongside,
waving back. (They say time passes only through our minds.)

Maybe it's enough, what we experience. There aren't many points of
            reference
in the Schubert, but there are some: your easy rhythms, my disequilibrium.
Music brings time close to us.
Gauguin sought a special blue for the Tahitians, whose nakedness had
            taken
mystery from sex, making men and women less different, less desperate.
(Does the natural teach us only the stupidity of our imaginations?) At noon,
office workers gather on the rooftops, women with women, men with men.

Real or imagined, time is here. (Where does it go when it passes?)
At times, only improbable things feel right. Your train this evening
may have disappeared into the Bermuda Triangle.
Night arrives, emptying the street. The sky gets bigger; feelings
feel like ravings. Why spend time being composed? The pointillists
saw truth in bits and pieces, painted big, shimmering bafflements
            from little flickerings. On a day like this, why wish for more?

I've wished at times to live at the extremes; fought time with excess;
sought, with no wish to find, a balance; gone too far and paid with time.

Time moved on, overcoming everything. The sun and moon shot back
and forth like shuttles, brilliantly repeating blues and greens
and other things that held on to their beauty: Van Gogh's olive trees
resembling men and the enigmatic women of Gauguin.

You're late. In the sixth grade, gripped by symmetry-passion, I moved
my arms in synchrony. When "death" came up, I had to find a reference to
 "life."
My eyes were nature's eyes, my arms, the pendulum that swung past day
 and night.
Gauguin went to Tahiti to create Paradise. Where was I then, what news
raced to me? Measuring in light years, it's one second to the moon. Where
 are you?

I re-do the Schubert. Nature snaps her fingers. Hours go, days, months.
Is it too late to wonder about time? (I've been acting like today was
special.) It's possible, after all, that the universe just happens once,
that the unpaintable expression on your face just happens once.
 The table's set for when you come home from the universe. Are
 you stuck
in a Van Gogh landscape with a Gauguin woman? Maybe it's enough,
 what we can do,
enough to explain the universe mathematically, like music, or place
a green beside a blue, or wait in an essentially natural world
under great artistic pressure. If this were Paris,
we'd be having croissants soon. Happiness is in the present tense.
Is it beginning? Do we need to be intimate with forever?

No train has to stop at 8:00 here, but there's someone waiting for it
whose life requires direction. Without events, time lacks definition.
You return. I resume, unsure of sequences. When exactly did you vanish?
Does light flow out of stars or stream into them? Do we know anything?
 Schubert backwards isn't Schubert. You have finished being gone.

Time Problem

The problem
of time.   Of there not being
enough of it.

My girl came to the study
and said Help me;
I told her I had a time problem
which meant:
I would die for you but I don't have ten minutes.
Numbers hung in the math book
like motel coathangers.   The Lean
Cuisine was burning
like an ancient city: black at the edges,
bubbly earth tones in the center.
The latest thing they're saying is lack
of time might be
a "woman's problem." She sat there
with her math book sobbing—
(turned out to be prime factoring: whole numbers
dangle in little nooses)
Hawking says if you back up far enough
it's not even
an issue, time falls away into
'the curve' which is finite,
boundaryless. Appointment book,
soprano telephone—
(beep End beep went the microwave)

The hands fell off my watch in the night.
I spoke to the spirit
who took them, told her: Time is the funniest thing
they invented. Had wakened from a big
dream of love in a boat—
No time to get the watch fixed so the blank face

lived for months in my dresser,
no arrows
for hands, just quartz intentions, just the pinocchio
nose   (before the lie)
left in the center;   the watch
didn't have 20 minutes; neither did I.

My girl was doing
her gym clothes by herself;   (red leaked
toward black, then into the white
insignia)   I was grading papers,
heard her call from the laundry room:
Mama?
Hawking says there are two
types of it,
real and imaginary   (imaginary time must be
like decaf), says it's meaningless
to decide which is which
but I say: there was tomorrow-
and-a-half
when I started thinking about it; now
there's less than a day. More
done. That's
the thing that keeps being said. I thought
I could get more done as in:
fish stew from a book. As in: Versateller
archon, then push-push-push
the tired-tired around the track like a planet.
Legs, remember him?
Our love—when we stagger—lies down inside us . . .
Hawking says
there are little folds of time
(actually he calls them wormholes)
but I say:
there's a universe beyond

where they're hammering the brass cut-outs . . .
Push us out in the boat and leave time here—

(because: where in the plan was it written,
You'll be too busy to close parentheses,
the snapdragon's bunchy mouth needs water,
even the caterpillar will hurry past you?)

Pulled the travel alarm
to my face: the black
behind the phosphorous argument kept the dark
from being ruined. Opened
the art book
—saw the languorous wrists of the lady
in Tissot's "Summer Evening." Relaxed. Turning
gently. The glove
(just slightly—but still:)
"aghast";
opened Hawking, he says, time gets smoothed
into a fourth dimension
but I say
space thought it up, as in: Let's make
a baby space, and then
it missed. Were seconds born early, and why
didn't things unhappen also, such as
the tree became Daphne . . .

At the beginning of harvest, we felt
the seven directions.
Time did not visit us. We slept
till noon.
With one voice I called him, with one voice
I let him sleep, remembering
summer years ago,
I had come to visit him in the house of last straws
and when he returned

above the garden of pears, he said
our weeping caused the dew . . .

I have borrowed the little boat
and I say to him Come into the little boat,
you were happy there;

the evening reverses itself, we'll push out
onto the pond,
or onto the reflection of the pond,
whichever one is eternal—

The Possible Advantages of the Expendable Multitudes

There could be a quirk in the conception of time.
For instance, the brief slide of a single herring
In the sights of an ocean bird might be measured,
At the last moment, in a slow motion of milliseconds,
Each fin spread like a fan of transparent bones
Breaking gradually through the green sea, a long
And complete absorption in that one final movement
Of body and wave together. It could be lengthened
To last a lifetime.

Or maybe there is a strange particulate vision
Only possible in a colony of microscopic copepod
Swaying in and out of the sand eel's range, swallowed
Simultaneously by the thousands. Who knows
What the unseen see? There might be a sense
Of broadcast, a fulfillment of scattering felt
Among the barnacle larva, never achieved
By the predatory shag at the top of the chain.
And the meadow vole crouched immediately below
The barred owl must experience a sudden and unusual
Hard hold on the potential.

Death coming in numbers among the small and uncountable
Might be altered in its aspects. An invaded nest
Of tadpoles might perceive itself as an array of points
Lit briefly in a sparkling pattern of extinction
Along the shore. An endless variety of split-second
Scenes might be caught and held visible in the separate eyes
Of each sea turtle penned on the beach. Death,
Functioning in a thousand specific places at once,
Always completing the magnitude of its obligations,
Has never been properly recognized for its ingenuity.

We must consider the possibility
That from the viewpoint of a cluster of flagellates
We might simply appear to be possessed
By an awkward notion of longevity, a peculiar bias
For dying alone.

Persistence of Sound

A word is dead / When it is said, / Some say.

Sounds never die, some scientists say.
They fade from hearing, but keep rolling up
and down—smaller and smaller waves—forever.
Churchill orating, "We will never surrender,"
Nixon whining, "I am not a crook,"
Caruso singing *Vesti la giubba,*
Savanarola screaming "I want a hat
of blood!"—the right machine might amplify
the air-squiggles their voices made,
pluck them like worms from a wriggling pot.

I'd love to hear my dad ask Mom to marry him.
What did they sound like, conceiving me?
(Dad yelled, Mom whimpered, is my guess;
I'd love to be surprised.) I'd love to hear
Demosthenes's Greek, and the first Indo-European,
and what those Caucasians spoke
who left their perfect mummies in Xianping.
Anthropologists could hear the first human
step onto North America and know,
by plotting sound-decay, exactly when.

The air could prove a treasure trove dwarfing
Pompeii (Vesuvius still thundering;
Romans shrieking, buried alive.) Still, I hope
some sounds didn't survive: *You poison me!*
I picture Kevin when I come with you!
Maybe sound slops up and down just briefly,
then is cancelled out. Otherwise,
someday we'll buy tapes of Jurassic birds,
of trees toppling in forests with no one to hear,
the crash retained in air the way a gold

bracelet torn by a Viking off an Irish
arm and melted down, retains traces
of serpent form, and the soft freckled skin
that warmed it, that the girl passed down to me—
the way a pterosaur's atoms (returned
to earth, re-used over and over) retain
in their vibrations every fish it ate, the squawks
it made feeding its young, the splash
when its heart—so like mine—stopped
and dropped into the undulating sea.

Vespers

In my ear the evening hush rustles
like grasshopper bones—and Augustine speaks to me
of the "fair harmony of time."

Over the broken Divide, western clouds slog along
like tired festival workers in a winepress, stunned
on color. Everywhere, the Hieronymus Bosch country.

"Your bones snow into the earth,
isn't that both sides of the question?"

And now the dark begins to develop
further back than the pyramids, hyper-considerably.
One by one its infinities gleam, printing the blood
between my every two pulses. This thick stellar traffic
my past always shoots me among—where the simplest words
like "In the beginning . . ." explode.

Dream shrapnel, the brain—its light at this hour
always frantic with meditations on some One
as the grenade of its choice not to exist
for billions of years, if ever. Out there
burning incomparable tracks.

"How do you take your daisies?"
"Oh, radiant, I guess. Through the eyeballs
like nails. Like this."

MICHAEL L. JOHNSON

Fibonacci Time Lines

cat's
claw's
curl, pine-
cone's swirl, goat's
horn's turn, nautilus'
shell's homing out, pineapple's whorl,
sneezewort's branchings, hair's twist, parrot's beak's
      growth, elephant's
tusk's curve, monkey's tail's spiral, cochlea's whirl
      of sound, Vitruvius' analogies,
Parthenon's geometry, logarithms' golden sections, time's
      way through form, mind's acceleration on its helical
      vector to death . . .

4

Matter

You look, and that's just where, of course, the problem starts . . .

M. L. WILLIAMS

JORIE GRAHAM

from Sir Francis Bacon's Novum Organum

<small>(AN ADAPTATION)</small>

Let the first motion be that of the resistance of matter, which exists in every particle, and completely prevents its annihilation; so that no conflagration, weight, pressure, violence, or length of time can reduce even the smallest portion of matter to nothing, or prevent it from being something, and occupying some space, and delivering itself (whatever straits it be put to), by changing its form or place, or, if that be impossible, remaining as it is; nor can it ever happen that it should either be nothing or nowhere.

Let the second motion be that which we term the motion of connection, by which bodies do not allow themselves to be separated at any point from the contact of another body, delighting, as it were, in the mutual connection and contact. This is called by the schools a motion to prevent a vacuum. It takes place when water is drawn up by suction or a syringe, the flesh by cupping, or when the water remains without escaping from perforated jars, unless the mouth be opened to admit the air—and innumerable instances of a like nature.

Let the third be that which we term the motion of liberty, by which bodies strive to deliver themselves from any unnatural pressure or tension, and to restore themselves to the dimensions suited to their mass.

Let the fourth be that which we term the motion of matter, and which is opposed to the last; for in the motion of liberty, bodies abhor, reject, and avoid a new size or volume, or any new expansion or contraction (for these different terms have the same meaning), and strive, with all their power, to rebound and resume their former density; on the contrary, in the motion of matter, they are anxious to acquire a new volume or dimension, and attempt it willingly and rapidly, and occasionally by a most vigorous effort, as in the example of gunpowder.

Let the fifth be that which we term the motion of continuity. We do not understand by this simple and primary continuity with any other body (for that is the motion of connection), but the continuity of a particular body in itself, for it is most certain that all bodies abhor a solution of continuity, some more and some less, but all partially.

Let the sixth be that which we term the motion of acquisition, or the motion of need. It is that by which bodies placed amongst others of a heterogeneous and, as it were, hostile nature, if they meet with the means or opportunity of avoiding them, and uniting themselves with others of a more analogous nature, even when these latter are not closely allied to them, immediately seize and, as it were, select them, and appear to consider it as something acquired (whence we derive the name), and to have need of these latter bodies. For instance, gold, or any other metal in leaf, does not like the neighborhood of air; if, therefore, they meet with any tangible and thick substance (such as the finger, paper, or the like) they immediately adhere to it, and are not easily torn from it. Paper, too, and cloth, and the like, do not agree with the air, which is inherent and mixed in their pores. They readily, therefore, imbibe water or other liquids, and get rid of the air. Sugar, or a sponge, dipped in water or wine, and though part of it be out of the water or wine, and at some height above it, will yet gradually absorb them.

Let the seventh be that which we term the motion of greater congregation, by which bodies are borne towards masses of a similar nature, for instance, heavy bodies towards the earth, light to the sphere of heaven.

Let the eighth be that which we term the motion of lesser congregation, by which the homogeneous parts in any body separate themselves from the heterogeneous and unite together, and whole bodies of a similar substance coalesce and tend towards each other, and are sometimes congregated, attracted, and meet, from some distance.

Let the ninth be the magnetic motion, which, although of the nature of that last mentioned, yet, when operating at great distances, and on great masses, deserves a separate inquiry.

Let the tenth motion be that of avoidance, or that which is opposed to the motion of lesser congregation, by which bodies, with a kind of antipathy, avoid and disperse, and separate themselves from, or refuse to unite themselves with others.

Let the eleventh motion be that of assimilation, or self-multiplication, or simple generation.

Let the twelfth motion be that of excitement.

Let the thirteenth motion be that of impression, which is also a species of motion of assimilation, and the most subtle of diffusive motions.

Let the fourteenth motion be that of configuration or position, by which bodies appear to desire a peculiar situation, collocation, and configuration with others, rather than union or separation. This is a very abstruse notion and has not been well investigated.

Let the fifteenth motion be that of transmission or of passage, by which the powers of bodies are more or less impeded or advanced by the medium, according to the nature of the bodies and their effective powers, and also according to that of the medium. For one medium is adapted to light, another to sound, another to heat and cold, another to magnetic action, and so on. . . .

Let the sixteenth be that which we term the royal or political motion, by which the predominant and governing parts of any body check, subdue, reduce, and regulate the others, and force them to unite, separate, stand still, move, or assume a certain position, not from any inclination of their own, but according to a certain order, and as best suits the convenience of the governing part, so that there is a sort of dominion and civil government exercised by the ruling part over its subjects.

Let the seventeenth position be the spontaneous motion of revolution.

Let the eighteenth motion be that of trepidation.

It is the motion of an (as it were) eternal captivity.

When bodies, for instance, being placed not altogether according to their nature, constantly tremble, and are restless, not contented with their position.

Such is the motion of the heart and pulse of animals.

And it must necessarily occur in all bodies which are situated in a mean state, between convenience and inconvenience.

So that being removed from their proper position, they strive to escape, are repulsed, and again continue to make the attempt. . . .

JORIE GRAHAM

from Sir Francis Bacon's Novum Organum

(AN ADAPTATION)

We took a metal bell, of a light and thin sort, such as is used for salt-cellars, and immersed it in a basin of water, so as to carry the air contained in its interior down with it to the bottom of the basin. We had first, however, placed a small globe at the bottom of the basin, over which we placed the bell. The result was, that if the globe were small compared with the interior of the bell, the air would contract itself, and be compressed without being forced out, but if it were too large for the air readily to yield to it, the latter became impatient of the pressure, raised the bell partly up, and ascended in bubbles.

We took a glass egg, with a small hole at one end; we drew out the air by violent suction at this hole, and then closed the hole with the finger, immersed the egg in water, and then removed the finger. The air being constrained by the effort made in suction, and dilated beyond its natural state, and therefore striving to recover and contract itself (so that if the egg had not been immersed in water, it would have drawn in the air with a hissing sound), now drew in a sufficient quantity of water to allow the air to recover its former dimensions.

We took a leaden globe . . .

On First Reading Particle Physics

About this time last year in March, the sky
was cold as kings; it rippled with *fiat lux*
and loomed behind trees black as blackguards.
It looked to be a philosopher's light that pried
for foothold on the cleavage face of a cliff.
Several neap tides later and having read
particle physics I know—you may already know,
but I didn't—there's no there there,
only a tendency to exist, and nature's
rock bottom fluxes to the shape of the query.

As we penetrate into the matter
she will not show basic building blocks,
only a web of relations that includes
the one who wonders in wavelike patterns.
And so to speak of particle X, gracefully
tracking across a photographic plate,
arcing cannily like frost on panes,
is at once to speak of the viewer, the one
holding the plate, the one saying pretty.

Up here in the macroscopic world,
we ride a Naples yellow van, pale as cake.
We might lob at the van some question,
but see how like a jerry-built egg it is;
the interior will be warm from sun
beading in windows with open curtains,
and what we ask is to trespass here,
on a plywood floor cushioned with our flesh,
until familiar heroes chunk the sky
and the highway darkens to huckleberry.

The Uncertainty Principle

You never know, and that's about the size
      of all these questions
Asked of matter. Matter never lies;
      it makes suggestions,
Hints at what it is, or where, or when,
      if one concedes
That time is not a particle, a spin
      each chronon bleeds
Across the vast continuum. You look,
      and that's just where,
Of course, the problem starts—your look
      that tries to swear
Allegiance to impartiality
      unburdened by
A metaphysic. A multiplicity
      of guesses ties
A knot around (just *where*) the answer hides,
      the way a lyric
Bends its words around a silence. To pride
      oneself on Phyrric
Wins against blank ignorance is vain.
      The stars shine on
And, outside, bluebirds argue in the vine;
      They know it's dawn.

Neutrinos

rush through the dribble of peach
at the baby's lips,
bowls of pabulum, raisins and milk
mixing with grit
from the split of beginnings.
Wraiths to our shadows,
they drift towards the teeter-totter
mounted in the yard.
Unseen, they'll propel
through that baby grown stooped,
quaint with her worm-brown spots
and wisps of hair.
They'll watch her track
powdery stipples in a telescope.
And lulled by dust
from the blaze of our star,
we'll have blinked our names away,
charged in a web
of spinning jots.
You, me, we, them. It.

Cosmic Gall

Every second, hundreds of billions of these neutrinos pass
through each square inch of our bodies, coming from above
during the day and from below at night, when the sun is
shining on the other side of the earth!

From "An Explanatory Statement on Elementary Particle Physics"
by M. A. Ruderman and A. H. Rosenfeld, in *American Scientist.*

Neutrinos, they are very small.
    They have no charge and have no mass
And do not interact at all.
The earth is just a silly ball
    To them, through which they simply pass,
Like dustmaids down a drafty hall
    Or photons through a sheet of glass.
    They snub the most exquisite gas,
Ignore the most substantial wall,
    Cold-shoulder steel and sounding brass,
Insult the stallion in his stall,
    And, scoring barriers of class,
Infiltrate you and me! Like tall
And painless guillotines, they fall
    Down through our heads into the grass.
At night, they enter at Nepal
    And pierce the lover and his lass
From underneath the bed—you call
    It wonderful: I call it crass.

The Woman Painting Crates

> *All structure is a manifestation of underlying process.*
> Fritjof Capra

The day after the physicist speaks
I paint crates frosty berry blue
as if to confirm they are solid

or else to admire their masterful
illusion—there is no solid stuff
in these structures made of particles

no one can touch or stop
from spinning at fierce velocities.
I am mostly empty space

and for an instant the terror
of flying apart rushes through me
like a close call on the interstate.

Even this body, good paint,
which I am finally comfortable riding
is made of nothing but process,

is no different from the crate
or the atoms of hydrogen in this brush.
Once all things could be understood

if broken into smaller pieces.
Now, the physicist tells me, matter
disappears into haloes

of transforming unexpected
connectedness. I am more than
that accidental assembly—

but to say it, is like trying
to copy the curved face of Earth
on a flat map. If I could know

that process of energy in myself
I could know what continues.
But knowing is what I try

to train myself out of,
painting these crates a new color
closer to a certain blue.

Giving In

At 1.4 million atmospheres
xenon, a gas, goes metallic.
Between squeezed single-bevel
diamond anvils jagged bits
of graphite shot with a YAG
laser form spherules. No one
has seen liquid carbon. Try
to imagine that dense world
between ungiving diamonds
as the pressure mounts, and
the latticework of a salt
gives, nucleating at defects
a shift to a tighter order.
Try to see graphite boil. Try
to imagine a hand, in a press,
in a cellar in Buenos Aires,
a low-tech press, easily
turned with one hand, easily
cracking a finger in another
man's hand, the jagged bone
coming through, to be crushed
again. No. Go back, up, up
like the deep diver with
a severed line, up, quickly,
to the orderly world of ruby
and hydrogen at 2.5 megabar,
the hydrogen coloring near
metallization, but you hear
the scream in the cellar, don't
you, and the diver rises too fast.

Amor Fati

In a world without purpose there are no accidents.
Consider the tragedy of a cup of coffee
When abandoned on a counter or a table.
Unless hit by an elbow or a hockey stick,
We know in an hour it'll be cold.
But no matter how we calculate
Clay mug, formica, air warm or chilly,
Silverware spoon tilting in it,
Sugar, milk, barometric pressure,
Temperature of everything at the onset
Of its adventure, a million factors
And the exact formulas of being
Intrinsic to each and their every interaction,
We can't predict, not with the world's
Biggest computer, Cyber or Cray, the heat
Of that steaming beverage a moment
Or full minute after it gets set down.
And yet if due to the erratic essence
Of nature, its tendency to balk
Or accelerate, you have to sip it
And guess, you know in an hour, untouched,
It'll be cold. This is what Freud called
Reality. He meant death. Of course
The world can intervene. If an elbow
Or hockey stick, or someone like me
With Siberian genes, who likes it hot,
Swallows or spills the whole cup,
This is no accident. This is fate
Saying love it, or mop it up.

Saliences

Consistencies rise
and ride
the mind down
hard routes
    walled
with no outlet and so
to open a variable geography,
    proliferate
possibility, here
is this dune fest
    releasing
mind feeding out,
gathering clusters,
fields of order in disorder,
where choice
can make beginnings,
    turns,
    reversals,
where straight line
and air-hard thought
can meet
unarranged disorder,
    dissolve
before the one event that
creates present time
in the multi-variable
    scope:
a variable of wind
among the dunes,
making variables
of position and direction and sound
of every reed leaf
and bloom,

running streams of sand,
winding, rising, at a depression
falling out into deltas,
weathering shells with blast,
striking hiss into clumps of grass,
against bayberry leaves,
        lifting
the spider from footing to footing
hard across the dry even crust
toward the surf:
wind, a variable, soft wind, hard
steady wind, wind
shaped and kept in the
bent of trees,
the prevailing dipping seaward
of reeds,
the kept and erased sandcrab trails:
wind, the variable to the gull's flight,
how and where he drops the clam
and the way he heads in, running to loft:
wind, from the sea, high surf
and cool weather;
from the land, a lessened breakage
and the land's heat:
wind alone as a variable,
as a factor in millions of events,
leaves no two moments
on the dunes the same:
        keep
free to these events,
bend to these
changing weathers:
multiple as sand, events of sense
alter old dunes
of mind,

release new channels of flow,
free materials
to new forms:
wind alone as a variable
takes this neck of dunes
out of calculation's reach:
come out of the hard
routes and ruts,
pour over the walls
of previous assessments: turn to
the open,
the unexpected, to new saliences of feature.

*   *   *

The reassurance is
that through change
continuities sinuously work,
cause and effect
    without alarm,
gradual shadings out or in,
motions that full
    with time
do not surprise, no
abrupt leap or burst: possibility,
with meaningful development
of circumstance:

when I went back to the dunes today,
    saliences,
congruent to memory,
spread firmingly across my sight:
the narrow white path
rose and dropped over
grassy rises toward the sea:
sheets of reeds,
tasseling now near fall,

filled the hollows
with shapes of ponds or lakes:
bayberry, darker, made wandering
chains of clumps, sometimes pouring
into heads, like stopped water:
    much seemed
constant, to be looked
forward to, expected:
from the top of a dune rise,
look of ocean salience: in
    the hollow,
where a runlet
    makes in
at full tide and fills a bowl,
extravagance of pink periwinkle
along the grassy edge,
and a blue, bunchy weed, deep blue,
deep into the mind the dark blue
    constant:
minnows left high in the tide-deserted pocket,
    fiddler crabs
bringing up gray pellets of drying sand,
disappearing from air's faster events
at any close approach:
certain things and habits
    recognizable as
having lasted through the night:
though what change in
a day's doing!
desertions of swallows
    that yesterday
ravaged air, bush, reed, attention
in gatherings wide as this neck of dunes:
now, not a sound
or shadow, no trace of memory, no remnant
    explanation:

summations of permanence!
where not a single single thing endures,
the overall reassures,
deaths and flights,
shifts and sudden assaults claiming
limited orders,
the separate particles:
earth brings to grief
much in an hour that sang, leaped, swirled,
yet keeps a round
    quiet turning,
beyond loss or gain,
beyond concern for the separate reach.

RONALD WALLACE

Chaos Theory

1. Sensitive Dependence on Initial Conditions

For want of a nail the shoe was lost,
for want of a shoe the horse was lost,
and so on to the ultimate loss—a battle,
a world. In other words, the breeze
from this butterfly's golden wings
could fan a tsunami in Indonesia
or send a small chill across the neck
of an old love about to collapse in Kansas
in an alcoholic stupor—her last.
Everything is connected. Blame it on
the butterfly, if you will. Or the gesture
thirty years ago, the glance across
the ninth-grade auditorium floor,
to the girl who would one day be your
lover, then ex-lover, then the wind
that lifts the memory's tsunami,
the mare of the imagination, bolting,
the shoe that claps the nail down on
your always already unending dream.

2. Love's Discrete Nonlinearity

No heart's desire is repeatable, or,
therefore, predictable. If a few hungry foxes
gorge on a large population of rabbits,
the population of foxes increases
while that of the rabbits declines,
until some point of equilibrium is passed
and the foxes begin to vanish with
the depleted supply of rabbits, and then
the rabbits multiply, like rabbits. And so on.
The ebb and flow of desire and fulfillment

is a story as old as the world. So,
if I loved you, finally, too much, until
you began to disappear, and I followed,
would you theoretically return to love
repeatedly again? There are forces so small
in our story of foxes and rabbits
no Malthus could ever account for them.
Whole species daily disappear, intractable
as weather. Or think of a continent's
coastlines, their unmeasurable eddies
and whorls: infinite longings inscribed
by finite space and time,
the heart's intricate branchings.

3. Strange Attractors

Our vision is simply not large or small enough
to encompass love's fractal geometry.
Who can know the motion of whorl within whorl
entrancing that paradoxical coastline, the changing
habitat of rabbits, the possibility that,
in the clockwork attraction of the solar
system, some heavenly body may not appear
every few million years, to throw all our
calculations asunder? Which says something
for randomness, which has its own hopeful
story. It's just that the patterns of love
and loss are so limitless that chaos
makes its own beautiful picture in which
we are neither (for all our grand needs
and egos) first cause nor unrepeatable.
We are uniquely strange attractors, love's
pendulum point or arc, time's shape or fancy,
in a system with its own logic, be it
the cool elegance of eternity, or
the subatomic matrix of creation and decay.

Dark Matter

It's good to stand at the head of the tram;
it seems like facing fate. Men and children
stand there mostly, next to the brochure rack
and the older women sit on cushions while
the blond, ski-sunburned guide points out
formations on our left: Red Dog Rock (sandstone
forehead furrowed like a basset hound's)
and KT-22, so mathematical. Below us, mixed
conifers, dazzling hurt granite from which
the basalt flowed, and with us the same confusion
as we rise; joy and terror have the same source.

At the top, families head up the rough trail
to mildly dirty patches of old snow. It's summer;
they want to touch it. Two red-haired boys
throw snowballs at their father. Some women
stand with their hands on their hips,
gazing eastward through infinite space.
Brewer's blackbirds land hysterically among
a mile of newly blossomed mules-ears,
and on a cliff's face, a patch of ice shaped
like a sombrero; today nature seems male.
More forevers and more forevers, and then—

I want to see everything but they say now
most of the universe is hidden;
they call what we can't see dark matter,
those particles straining unprovenly through
what is, sucking gravity from the edge
of galaxies. They're trying to find just one
speck of it . . . Why am I thrilled by the idea
that this hurried thing cannot be caught?
That this huge mountain's filled with it,
billions of it going through me every second.
That as I sit on this log, slightly drunk

from the high altitude, looking at sidalcea
in the sun, in awe of moraines, that
I'm being hit with it. Why love the thought
of being struck by a dark thing clean through.
That the little family throwing snow now
in their innocent ways are being penetrated
by an opposite, the main universe, a huge
allegorical black urgency—and we are nothing
but a rind of consciousness, a mild
excess, a little spare color, and not just us,
the thistles and the asters and the blackbirds . . .

Of course this happened at the start of time,
something had to pull away, and I've been trying
to love the missingness in the middle,
the caves of wounded magic; I've studied
the old terrors every day, the brightness
of the world, have loved the random causes,
have learned the kinds of pain in California,
have known the desire to make from pain
some words that would be beautiful and torn—
and now, I want this wholeness. Here,
the blackbirds swarm upward, and the chipmunk

with one-and-a-half brown stripes takes off
with a prize; the red-haired family hurries
toward the tram under the smooth white ear
of the radar. The mountain seems to push up
through us, asking us to keep its hurt.
Today it seems possible to welcome
wounded matter; the ski-lift chairs,
which have lurched forward, being repaired
all afternoon, guard their incompleteness.
Each black, numbered frame pauses till its turn
then offers its own darkness a ride.

Sum

The scientific corruption arises from the method . . .
of isolating parts of the whole in order to understand
them. This has made us destroyers of Nature.

Bryan Appleyard, *Understanding the Present:*
Science and the Soul of Modern Man

Early atomists like Lucretius believed in unity,
seeking not to dissect the world but to imagine it.
To account for difference, one theory held
that matter was composed, in varying degrees, of
mixtures of the elements—dust, rain, wind, flame—
combining, recombining, so as to be conserved,
eternal as we are not.
Ever more accurate, we weigh the world for proof,
the balance pole with its brass pans, oldest of our tools.

But what if matter, weighed piece by piece,
doesn't add up to a whole we can describe?
If, proceeding from the known, we meet
not the unknown but the unknowable?

In Memling's painting *The Last Judgment* it's no scientist
but Michael the Archangel, deputy of God,
who does the weighing, counts the bodies,
naked and strangely small, praying, crawling, buckling
backward before his sheathed and gleaming power.

5

Heavenly Bodies

Who can envision all of heaven trembling . . .

PATTIANN ROGERS

The Pieces of Heaven

No one alone could detail that falling—the immediate
Sharpening and blunting of particle and plane,
The loosening, the congealing of axis
And field, the simultaneous opening and closing
Composing the first hardening of moment when heaven first
    broke
From wholeness into infinity.

No one alone could follow the falling
Of all those pieces gusting in tattered
Layers of mirage like night rain over a rocky hill,
Pieces cartwheeling like the red-banded leg
Of the locust, rolling like elk antlers dropping
After winter, spiraling slowly like a fossil of squid
Twisting to the bottom of the sea, pieces lying toppled
Like bison knees on a prairie, like trees of fern
In a primeval forest.

And no one could remember the rising
Of all those pieces in that moment, pieces shining
Like cottonwood dust floating wing-side up
Across the bottomland, rising like a woman easily
Lifting to meet her love, like the breasting,
The disappearing surge and scattering crest of fire
Or sea blown against rock, bannered like the quills
Of lionfish in their sway, like the whippling stripe
Of the canebrake rattler under leaves.

Who can envision all of heaven trembling
With the everlasting motion of its own shattering
Into the piece called honor and the piece
Called terror and the piece called death and the piece
Tracing the piece called compassion all the way back
To its source in that initial crimp of potential particle
Becoming the inside and outside called matter and space?

And no one alone can describe entirely
This single piece of heaven partially naming its own falling
Or the guesswork forming the piece
That is heaven's original breaking, the imagined
Piece that is its new and eventual union.

LEN ROBERTS

Learning the Stars

Giant blue stars, yellows, and smaller reds
    whirled
across the seventh-grade blackboard
to form a flying horse and dogs, dippers,
Andromeda chained to a sea rock, Perseus's belt
cinched tight as Ann Harding's black patent leather strap,
Ronny Michaels whispering to Karen Awlen that he'd like
    to show her the stars from Canal Road,
Richie Reese staring off into space,
the braces on his legs wobbling as he clacked
to the board to circle the three stars of Polaris,
    Castor's six,
reciting the light years' distance to Antares,
telling us the ancients believed they were ruled
    by the stars
before he hobbled back to his desk.
    Alpheratz, Algol, Capella,
stars we traced and cut out on stiff
    construction paper,
brushed with fluorescent paints,
stars I carried home and set like sequins
    on my bedroom ceiling,
imagining the lines that made them figures
    I could comprehend
when I lay sleepless, my older brother's
    madness
glowing beside me in a cluster of light,
my younger brother jerking off every night,
red Aldebaran gleaming down on us from
    the Bull's eye
as I wrapped myself in the black cloak
    which made me invisible,
the Pole Star burning where my heart had been,

each star a cell in my space-darkened body,
star trails crisscrossing even then from my mind
    to my balls,
my fingers burning, my eyes burning in that field
    of flames,
the Star of Betrayal marked in ash on my forehead,
the Star of Hope flickering in my throat
where the names took shape in the absence of space,
    Harp, Bow, Sailing Ship,
pinpoints of light I could travel by, clear, bright,
    and fixed.

Stars

I sit and rock my son to sleep. It rains
and rains. Such as we are
both asleep, we swim past the stars,
bad stars of disaster, good stars of the backbone

of night. We know these stars as they are
and as we'd wish them to be, Milky Way,
Dog and Bear, hydrogen and helium, the 92
elements which make all we know of beauty.

We know nothing of angular size or
of the inverse square law of the propagation
of light, and swim through a cold, thin
gas, between and among the stars,

which swim likewise between two creations
like children who know sleep intimately.

*   *   *

First the collapse of the interstellar gasses,
then the final collapse of the luminous stars
like eyes turning backward in their sockets
returning the atoms they have synthesized

back into space, to dust, back to what they were.
We look from some kind of opening to nothing.
We locate the red giant and the dwarf star
for nothing. They are going away—

their explosions from within and their luster,
their mixed-up views on time and space.
I know that those I love are some
of the falling objects, and those dark waves
rise toward us from the past, dark
that falls with any particle of light.

Astrology

It's so clear tonight, and calm,
that if I stepped outside,
and raised my head, I imagine
I could see the silver

chest hairs of Orion,
the hummingbird tattoo upon
the outside of his thigh.
And further back, the unfathomable

dark, which makes it possible for him
to draw his bow,
and gives him room to choose
a target for the night.

So I remember the luxury of what
I've had the poor taste in the past
to call, sometimes, our loneliness,
which is the absence of others

who have left us stranded here,
with only oxygen to breathe
and nothing more than time
to breathe it in.

And I honor, for a moment, the million
things forgotten, the things
which have so graciously
forgotten me—the bulging

saddlebags of history, the myriad, self-cancelling
blunders and eurekas
of fathers and mothers
of fathers and mothers and fathers—

who have handed down something
of tremendous importance

by handing down nothing
but plenty of quiet and dark.

And in the fields of sky above our houses,
these well-lit
hieroglyphics, open to
our own interpretation.

Ploughing the Dark

FOR LES BRILL

Isn't it enough that a forest stands
at the edge of a man being eaten
by a lit cigarette? His face disappears,
reappears. His eyes have travelled here
from bouillon. A squirrel's shadow streams
down an oak, a few frogs creak like chairs.
One barleycorn grit—on the road
since when?—strikes air like a match,
its meteor ploughing the dark, fading
on retinal nerve. He has seen a boulder-size
hunk, come to earth for an Arizona blacksmith
to anvil away on for years, malleable
as nail metal. You could stipulate burial,
he supposes, clenching bits of it
in your right hand. Perhaps shoe a horse.
As if there were any other way.

In the Smithsonian, an Egyptian crisp
as winter sycamore leaf before it floats off
is lying alone in his glass case, a prim card
listing stomach contents recovered—some granules,
apparently wheat, having swum like Jonah
through the painted dreaming of tomb walls
onto this bowl.

Once a horticulturist from Japan
showed him slides of a lotus recollecting itself
from seed 1,800 years old, waiting
in certain layerings of Honshu peat
for an audience. As if out of night sky
the petals open, perfectly formed.

Imponderable tonnages all around, hurtling,
burning. He lights a fresh cigarette,
then returns his look to gardening the stars.
Natal physics, brilliancies his eye
can never take in, except finally.
What percent has consciousness? His estimate
trudges miles, carrying a decimal point
to its blind address. 10 to the 18th?
Even less? Meanwhile the city's houses
are tired. In some of them, hovering
cantaloupe rind by the sink are fruit flies
whose forelegs end in nerve distinguishing
5 different sugars. But the houses
are tired, the houses are weary,
and the people are bored.

A Moon Eclipsed

"You see," the learned astronomer said to us,
"When instruments were born into the world,
Map, globe and chart, astrolabe and orrery,
And after them the planetarium
Projecting the stars as from inside the eyes,
They brought along out of the earlier earth
A grand consortium of remaindered gods
With their associated nymphs and satyrs,
Centaurs and giants, which only slowly faded;
But when that chimaeric thereomorphic chorus
Ceased from their song and presently disappeared,
The telescopes would work as well, the maps
Still better, if not adorned with giant forms,
And we were left alone with nameless mind
Projecting its immense geometries
At the speed of light, the limiting speed of time,
To the end of our more perfect understanding."

So when we stayed up all that night to see
(but was it seeing, or seeing's opposite?)
A second darkness move across the night,
We saw exactly what he said we should:
The transit of the Earth with Sun and Moon
Casting a shadow intercepted and cupped
(a small vanilla scoop in a cone of dark)
As of a golf ball sitting on a tee
So big as to conceal it from the ground
Till it fell off the other side and life
Continued on its ordinary course
As it had always done. We saw it with
Our stereoscopic, single-power eyes.

Looking Up at Night

It's awful stillness the moon feels, how the earth
wants it, that great, still, steady rock
floating serenely around. It knows it belongs
nearer its bright neighbor that shepherds it through
the sky. And the two begin to converge toward
the docking that will shatter history and bring new continents
hissing out of the sea, and erase with tide
and sand the old eternal cities and monuments and mountains.

LEN ROBERTS

Learning the Planets

The planets whirled across the blackboard
        all morning,
Saturn with its twelve rings,
        Jupiter with its belts,
red Mars, green Venus, the familiar
        blue earth
where we sat in that eighth-grade class
        learning light
years, eight light-minutes for the sun's rays
        to touch my arm,
Alpha Centauri 4.4 light-years away,
Betelgeuse, the giant red star in Orion's
        shoulder, 300,
Rigel, the blue giant in Orion's knee,
        540,
the vastness of blackness suddenly ours
while Richie Reese picked his nose
and lovely Karen Awlen hitched up her dress.
        Infinity and eternity
blurred by the sun in dull yellow chalk
as I felt the pull of the planets and their
        moons
hold me in my desk where carved hearts
        orbited
with the names of those I did not know,
        Jimmy loves Sue,
Tina and Barry circled by a ring of smoke
        drifting
up from a speeding Chevy, *I love my dog,*
        Snookie,
etched in small, straight lines by the inkwell.
        1944, 1946, 1950, '53, '56,
each year trailed names the way Halley's

comet trailed light that October morning,
and I carved *Lorraine, 1958*, with a crescent
     moon cupping it
while Sister Angelica told us Copernicus
     knew the earth was a wanderer,
Galileo the first to see the phases of Venus,
     sunspots,
telling us about the Black Hole that sucked
     all light into it,
spreading her black-winged arms and wrapping
     Margaret Blake
to show her what it was like, unfolding
     Margaret's chalk-white face
when she began to cry, the face that would begin
     to glow whiter
in a few years and then fade, cancer of the lungs
     they said
but we all knew it was the blackness she saw back
     in that class,
blackness revolving in Sister's heart,
blackness of distances we could not even imagine,
blackness we heard even then in Margaret's sobs while
     cosmic
clouds floated on the board with the label, *raw material*
     of creation,
where stars were born and died,
and planets whirled on their inevitable paths.

Heavenly Bodies

1

How the visiting schoolchildren must have
trembled in their adolescence
when Hilda Doolittle led them into the peerless room
of the Flower Observatory near Philadelphia
to gaze through the telescope
at the flat plain of stars.
They knew then that angels were frail
and pedestrian,
and carrying this revelation home,
opened *The Book of Knowledge*
to the "Things to Make and Things to Do" section
and constructed telescopes in their backyards.

2

In New Orleans a street peddler sold
glances through his telescope
outside Café du Monde, and in the swank hours,
people in evening clothes would fish
for dimes in their pockets
to look up at the moon caught in the sky
like café au lait inside a cup,
and when I looked, I saw,
for so little money,
that no one would ask me
to dance the two-step
under the artificial stars of the Blue Room.

3

My father taught me that the universe could move
in the ell of the dining room.
Turning an orange between his thumb and forefinger

before a light bulb, he made night fall
on the far side of the orange
where people slept in rice paper houses
after the Winding River banquets.
The shadows of the planets bobbed
on the walls of our house.
He was in charge of the Heavenly Bodies,
coming up the walk in midsummer to focus the sun
with a magnifying glass on a matchbook
until it flared through the centers of our lives.

Not much in my life has gone the way I wanted,
and I believe that we go a long time
under the earth without seeing.
My father's cataracts float
in formalin in the medicine cabinet,
though he can name the states in geographical order
and the constellations,
by picturing them in the darkness of his head.
He tells us that when he dies,
he will come in his pickup to drive us
to Emerald Mound
where the Big Dipper hangs over the oaks
and resurrection fern
like the tin cup we drank from at the cistern
the summer my mother lost her diamond
in the garden in a row of Kentucky Wonders.

Comet

The comet comes again.
Astronomer, tell when.

When ends its long eclipse?
Where meets the long ellipse?

Plot its explicit path
In geometric graph.

Trace its eccentric course
Through the curved universe.

Expound to us the law
By which we see again
The comet we first saw
As boys, now as old men.

BRUCE BERGER

Stellar Gothic

From the southern and Sagittarian
End of our galaxy
Comes a tale taken with barely
Imagined gravity.

A star stripped to its neutrons,
They say, is fatally linked
To an ever shrinking white dwarf
Whose flames are nearly extinct.

No ballroom binaries,
They've tightened their embrace
To a mere third of the distance
Between the moon and your face.

Every eleven minutes
Their X-ray pantomime
Executes a death spiral
Across the ice of spacetime.

The dwarf does most of the dying.
At random intervals
In their S/M infatuation
The neutron partner pulls

Pieces off the dwarf
On which its masses fatten,
A hundred thousand suns
In bites the size of Manhattan.

Even on earth they make waves,
Displaying some rather eerie
Twists of gravitation
Implied by the General Theory

Of Relativity and found
At last, although to be fair

Even Einstein never envisioned
So McCullers a pair.

Wider, sharper, deeper
The orbiting space probe delves
Into regions where we no longer
May care to project ourselves.

HE 2-104: A True Planetary Nebula in the Making

On the universal clock, Sagan tells us,
we are only moments old. And this
new crab-like discovery in Centaurus,
though older by far, is but
an adolescent going through a vital
if brief stage in the evolution
of interacting stars. I see it
starting its sidereal trek
through midlife, glowingly complex—
"a pulsating red giant" with a "small
hot companion" in tow—and think
of you and me that night in August
speeding across Texas in your red
Mustang convertible, enveloped in dust
and fumes, aiming for a motel bed,
settling instead for the backseat of the car,
arms and legs flailing in all directions,
but mostly toward heaven—and now
this cool red dude winking at me
through the centuries as if to say
I know, I know, sidling in closer
to his sidekick, shedding his garments,
shaking off dust, encircling
her small girth with a high-density
lasso of himself, high-velocity
sparks shooting from her ringed
body like crazy legs and arms until
at last, he's got his hot companion
in a classic hold and slowly,
in ecstasy, they take wing and
blaze as one across the Southern skies—
no longer crab but butterfly.

The North Star

See, it is the only one
that will not lie.
It is not tempted
to change like the others

that flicker to color
and disappear.
It has seen so much it knows
better than that.

It remembers the frailties
of being human
and becoming lost, all those
drowned ones it saw,

begging to the end for air,
or those claimed by
the woods who never again
would hear the human voice.

This star is the only one
that knows the importance
of position
in the flow of time and weather.

And that if you want
salvation, you will
look to it as the others did
and not ask it why.

PETER DILLINGHAM

Black Holes & Hologramarye

Star	Star's
Black	Black
Balled	Swan
By	(Song)
Space-Time	Hatching

Narcisse and the Black Hole

Having fallen to within $1.5(2GM/c^2)$
Of the black pool's center,
$Narcisse_{psi}$ reaches out,
Space-like through space
To possess a stranger,
An endless succession
Of casual passers by,

In ecstasy,
$Narcisse_n$ contemplates $Narcisse_1$,
A moment standing still forever
Transcending myth and dream,
Transcending the heavy scent,
The alien flesh of flowers,
A perfect image frozen forever
On the imperturbable surface
Of that dark mirror.

Holo-Caustic

Holo-Caustic—to view—in a dark room, hold a flashlight exactly illuminating the circle and read with a magnifying glass. This adds the approximate experience of the astronomer.

Left Hemisphere	Right Hemisphere
	the cell reacts
"It was visible by day	a glorious
Like Venus;"	sacrificial blossoming
Yang Wei-te	at 10,000 km/sec
Chief Computer of the Calendar,	phagocytic . . .
told the Emperor	triggered by
in July 1054;	contagion's spread
"pointed rays	a malignant thrusting forth
shot out from it	of virulent sentience
on all sides;	from long containment
the color was reddish-white . . ."	the cell reacts
	a glorious
In November, 1572, Tycho Brahe,	sacrificial blossoming
Astronomer of Florence,	at 10,000 km/sec
"saw,	phagocytic . . .
with inexpressible astonishment,	triggered by
near the zenith,	contagion's spread
in Cassiopeia,	a malignant thrusting forth
a radiant star	of virulent sentience
of extraordinary magnitude."	

Cosmological Holophrastics

1 — The Black Hole	2 — Matter Antimatter
Holehearted	Wholeface
Holotropic	Hollowface
Wholehog	
Whole-in-one	
Holeness	
Holiness	

Epitaph for a Star

Brief glory of your dusky spoondrift spiral,
Spendthrift giant of the blue flame of youth,
You left behind only singular chaos,
And a vortex of memory.

MICHAEL COLLIER

The Heavy Light of Shifting Stars

> *Some times the nite is the shape of a ear*
> *only it ain't a ear we know the shape of.*
> Russell Hoban, *Riddley Walker*

The huge magnanimous stars are many things.
At night we lower window shades
to mute the sparkling circuitry of the universe;
at day the sun's clear mist, like beautiful
cabinetry, shrouds the workings of the sky.

Everything is hidden, everything is apparent,
so that light coming toward us, held
in the faces of our old regrets, is blue;
while the light passing away, blurred
by our stationary focus, is red.

We cannot see these colors with our eyes,
just as we cannot feel the sun pushing the stars
outward or bending the paths of their light.
Years ago when the world was flat, and then even
when the world became round, light was light,

dark was dark, and now, now that the world
is almost nothing compared with all that is—
all that we know—light identifies each atom
of the universe, and darkness swallows stars
like a whirlpool at the heart of a galaxy.

The huge magnanimous stars are many things.
We look to the sky and ask, What has changed?
Everything. But nothing we can see, and our seeing
changes nothing, until we move, and moving
we become the light of our atoms moving.

6

Earth

*Thus stands my study from the
vials and furnaces of universal earth . . .*

LOREN EISELEY

Notes of an Alchemist

Crystals grow
        under fantastic pressures in the deep
                crevices and confines of
the earth.
        They grow by fires,
            by water trickling slowly
in strange solutions
        from the walls of caverns.
They form
        in cubes, rectangles,
         tetrahedrons,
                they may have
their own peculiar axes and
        molecular arrangements
          but they,
    like life,
      like men,
        are twisted by
the places into which
      they come.

I have only
    to lift my hands
      to see
the acid scars of old encounters.
          In my brain
as in the brains of all mankind
      distortions riot
and the serene
      quartz crystal of tomorrow is
most often marred
      by black ingredients
        caught blindly up,
but still

no one knows surely why
specific crystals meet
in a specific order.
Therefore we grasp
two things:
that rarely
two slightly different substances will grow
even together
but the one added ingredient
will transfigure
a colorless transparency
to midnight blue
or build the rubies' fire.
Further, we know
that if one grows a crystal
it should lie
under the spell of its own fluid
be
kept in a cool cavern
remote
from any violence or
intrusion from the dust.

So we
our wise men
in their wildernesses
have sought
to charm to similar translucence
the cloudy crystal of the mind.
We must then understand
that order strives
against the unmitigated chaos lurking
along the convulsive backbone of the world.
Sometimes I think that we
in varying degrees are grown
like the wild crystal,

            now inert,
now flashing red,
          but I
            within my surging molecules
by nature cling
         to that deep sapphire blue
              that marks the mind of one
long isolate
       who knows and does reflect
starred space and midnight,
        who conceives therefore
that out of order and disorder
          perpetually clashing and reclashing
come the worlds.
        Thus stands my study from the vials and furnaces
of universal earth. I leave it here
            for Heracleitus
if he comes again
        in the returnings of the Giant Year.

CARTER REVARD

This Is Your Geode Talking

I still remember ocean, how
she came in with all I wanted, how we opened
the hard shell we had made
of what she gave me and painted into
that lodge's white walls the shifting
rainbows of wave-spray—
I remember even the vague drifting
before the shell was made, my slow swimming
amidst the manna until I sank
down into stone, married, rooted there, joined
its stillness where the moving waters
would see us as the moon would lead them past.
Growing, I remember how softness
of pale flesh secreted the smooth hardness
of shell, how the gritty pain
was healed with rainbow tears
of pearl,
I remember dreaming
of the new creatures flying through air
as the sharks swam through ocean
hallucinating feathers and dinosaurs,
pterodactyls and archaeopteryxes,
great turquoise dragonflies
hovering, shimmering, hawking after the huge
mosquitoes fat with brontosaurus blood. And when
I died and the softness vanished inside
my shell and the sea flowed in I watched
it drying as the waters ebbed, saw how my boney whiteness held
at its heart the salty gel whose desire swelled
and grew and globed against the limey mud,
chalcedony selving edged and spiked its way
through dreams of being flowers trembling
against the wind, snowflakes falling

into a desert spring. But the rain
of limestone hardened round us and my walls
grew full of holes, I waked into
a continent of caves, a karst-land where
sweet water chuckled and trickled, siliceated through
my crevices as once the salty ocean had, and I felt
purple quartz-crystals blossom where
my pale flesh had been.
Then I knew my dream
was true, and I waited for
the soft hand to come down like a dream
and lift me into sunlight, give me there to diamond
saws that sliced me in two, to diamond dust that polished
my new selves of banded agate,
I let them separate and shelve them heavy
on either side of a word-hoard whose light leaves
held heavy thoughts between
the heavier, wiser, older lines of all
my mirrored selves, the wave-marks left
by snowflake-feathery amethyst
ways of being,
by all those words,
by the Word, made slowly,
slowly, in-
to Stone.

CARTER REVARD

Earth and Diamonds

How far from truth to beauty, say,
in diamonds?
Can we make either out of facts
put flatly, crunched together so their facets
crack light and spill
its rainbows over earth the way
plain carbon does when it is crushed into
a diamond, say?
A scientific fact was once
that stars made diamonds by their heavenly
"influence" acting deep within
the earth, mutating gunk
into bright gems;
but now it is a fact of science that earth
composes diamonds of itself—
and yet the earth itself was made
in superstars (another fact
of science, for the moment),
so that the house which stars once built
still crystallizes in the shape of stars, still
shines like them,
in language anyhow.
Of course
(you say) the earth, this common place, can't really shine.
But that's because we live too close to it:
the astronauts have seen
our muddy planet shine,
a blue star up in heaven.
That's what their eyes have seen:
their minds, of course, know very well it's not
a fact that's pure, it has
a flaw, depending on your point of view. It's air
that shines, and water mostly, earth

just holds these shining facts around
its heavy darkness.
So flights of angels, passing through our bodies,
may see a neutron shine
gemlike with facets, all the points of
inner structure netting
the radiant waves and fishing out
their rainbow messages of peace
from the God of Storms.
That, you'll say, is not
a fact—but if we just remove
the angels and insert
a physicist, you may allow
it is a fact though medaled
with metaphors and circumcised
by adjectives: . . . yes,
our physicist might say,
it is a fact
that neutrons have a structure,
and perhaps that each is like
a crystal, certainly
neutrons are being probed by beams of
some other particles,
and in the spectrum which comes back to us
from deep inside these specks of space
are messages concerning Universal
Creation and Apocalypse.
Thus far we state pure facts, although
they are imperfect when they're packed into
the seedy figures of our speech,
and blossom only in the arabesques
of math, which has no fruitful symbols for
Creation and Apocalypse except
a change of signs.
FACT meant SOMETHING MADE, in Roman mouths,

then English let it take the place of *TRUTH*.
Shakespeare was called, by Robert Greene,
"an absolute *FACTOTUM* in his own conceit."
He did it all,
that is, he *MADE* it all; instead of acting,
Shakespeare began to make the forms
for others' actions: yes, **FACTOTUM**,
that's the word.
People make diamonds now from coal, as easily
as they make perfume out
of oil, or pantyhose
from tar—
but diamonds we make
just as volcanoes did, with heat and pressure,
just as volcanoes were themselves
created by the moving
continents where the ocean's crust
dives under and the mountain-ship
floats over and begins to burn and thunder,
creating atmosphere, sunsets,
and diamonds in time.

And the male bowerbird creates his bower
to woo a mate, in fact the blue one chooses
only blue things to put in his,
he even mixes blue
paint and spreads it on his
bower's wall, using a piece of wood
or other brush to spread
the paint he's made from berries and
his way of seeing things.
But then, the fact is that
when once his mate is mated there
she leaves and builds her nest
and lays her eggs up in
some ordinary tree, and he just lets her go,

he takes no interest in the mortgage or the weather or the eggs, or in
those rising generations at their song,
he paints just what he sees, he makes
his gemlike house
of blue lights, keeps the species special and himself
fit to survive—and he's
a dinosaur, it seems, with warm blood, one
who put on feathers and survived—or so
facticians now assert as fact: the birds,
as Michael Castro says, are *DYNA-SOARS!*
If that is fact, we can no longer
believe that dinosaurs became extinct, just as we can
no longer hold that earth, not stars,
composes diamonds.
The trouble is, we keep exploding facts
into old myths, and then compressing myths
into new facts,
and so in this dark kaleidoscope
of headlined findings, what once was
crystal clear becomes too nebulous
to be believed,
—yet then becomes the evidence
that speaks of how our universe evolved,
as do the nebulae in space that once
were "clouds" and now are "ghosts"
of superstars that still broadcast the news
of brilliant bowers painted
upon the heavens long before
there was an earth
to sparkle bluely like a diamond in
the sky and make us wonder,
O twinkling little fact, just **WHAT**
you are: if true, how beautiful,
if beautiful, how true.

KAREN SWENSON

Dinosaur National

Jewelers,
in goggles and buttercup hardhats,
chip out a cameo of dinosaur bones—
vertebrae necklaces,
pelvic abstracts,
a baby stegosaurus skull
like a Disney dragon.
The entire mountain's flank
is chiseled out,
a bas-relief
of rainy day deaths on a sandbar
long before
the bingo card of our genes filled up.
Big in the hips herself,
it's not surprising
that earth would remember these.
But like a sentimental woman
who hoards
old dance cards
and ribbons from corsages,
she'll keep a feather
or the baby starfish
of a waterbird's footprint
one hundred fifty million years.
As I have treasured
the whorls of my son's day-old toes,
printed on his birth certificate,
so she preserved
four million years
two journeys taken on the same day
at Laetoli—
the long scratch
of a millipede's furrow in the dust
and a human romp of family
footprints, as they passed in the ashes.

RITA DOVE

The Fish in the Stone

The fish in the stone
would like to fall
back into the sea.

He is weary
of analysis, the small
predictable truths.
He is weary of waiting
in the open,
his profile stamped
by a white light.

In the ocean the silence
moves and moves

and so much is unnecessary!
Patient, he drifts
until the moment comes
to cast his
skeletal blossom.

The fish in the stone
knows to fail is
to do the living
a favor.

He knows why the ant
engineers a gangster's
funeral, garish
and perfectly amber.
He knows why the scientist
in secret delight
strokes the fern's
voluptuous braille.

PATTIANN ROGERS

Fossil Texts on Canyon Walls

1. Astrophysical Dynamics

There are fables and legends written
right on my bones, on the red grain
of my bones, visible plots, subplots,
captures and escapes, as decipherable
as black ink fictions scribed
on rolled parchments.

And finely needled tattooes—inked
permanently in trumpet creepers,
jungle canopies, moon-webs of winter,
bellflowers of blood—compose the inner
bowl of my skull. Ancient missals
and pre-earth percussions are recorded
inside every knuckle, engraved on the turns
and curls of my ankles and wrists.

By the spine, I am epic, its staff
and sway. I am an oratorio
of skeleton, an ave of stance. I bear
by body the chamber concert of birth,
the well-worn recital of death.

It's possible then for me to sink also,
a myth of sun buried, and to rise again
on earth, a parable spoken in stone
on a canyon wall.

I could truly relent now,
as if I believed bone were rock and rock
light and all boldering stars were fossils
of canyon histories, as if I knew stellar
stories were simply constellations
of the body and living blood were symphony,
all motions intergalactic, interheart,

just the same and as easy to negotiate
as the swing and pulse I might make
from one ringing refrain to the next.

2. This State of Stone

This canyon is the place for sleep,
the sleep of one watching himself
sleep, an immobile rock sleep filled
with the jumble of one's own stone
bones and the constant roaring of old
seas, a fossil tangle of sleep curled
and kept inside bright angel shale,
coconino sandstone, squeezed
among algal remnants, seed fern,
armored fish, worm burrows.

And this sleep is a familiar reading
of sleep, the descending and rising
layers of language, low violet and rose-
orange murmurs and striations, stratas
of predators and prey captured together,
the sleeping limestone cries and curses
of a million murders.

In this place one might sleep a wise
sleep, seeing with eyes opened by stone,
a sleep watching its own breaking
revelation, as looking in a mirror
one is suddenly broken in two.

If I falter, I must remember
that from this sleep engaged in the present
study of its own ancient sleeping,
one need never wake.

Rivers

Rain, sleet, snow, and hail's grand excess
over evaporation and the fine,
dense, constant transpiration of all flora,
provides the flow of rivers.
Earth is watered by the inequation:
Congo, Mississippi, Amazon,
Yangtze, Nile, Paraná,
Ob, Amur, Yanisei, and Lena.

Volumes could be written on the way
renowned and cryptic rivers flow:
their seasonal regimen,
occurrence and diastole of flood waves,
chemistry of river water, form of
river systems: snake and tree. And yet,
a poem needs restraint.
Take up the means at hand with a good will.

A river's organized in delicate balance,
self-formed, self-maintained, between
forces of erosion and resistance.
Curving the groove it runs along, it fashions
depth, and areal figure,
longitudinal profile, and cross section.
Equations show its equilibrium
studded with liquid, looped parameters:

Sheer (internal force tangential to
ideal cross sections); bedload (particles
from bed and bank transported by the river);
dissolved load (bedload made invisible).
Headwater pours across boulders and cobbles;
downstream material is
smoother, silt or silky clay. But scour
and fill tend on the average to balance.

A river overflows its banks in flood.
Everywhere, in rivers of all sizes,
bankfull stages happen once a year, or
once in two. The floodplain
has to drown biennially, and proves
inherent to a river.
What are we? Indeed, what are we not?
Ephemeral, the light dream of a shadow.

Despite the broad necessity of floods,
most fluvial work on landscape forms
stems from intermediate events:
a modest count of days of
intermediate flow or scour. Like love;
like ordinary science with its careful,
incomplete descriptions. *Let us be*
small in small things, great in greater things.

Nearly every natural channel snakes.
(Indeed, a river's rarely a straight line
longer than ten channel widths.)
Meandering or merely sinuous,
curves a channel carves
remain in constant ratio to its girth:
small channels wind in smaller, great in greater
curves. *The noblest element is water.*

Sinuosity's root cause is just
how water flows: hydro-
dynamics. Independent of its load,
any river slowly, surely migrates
laterally across the valley floor.
The laws of water run
beyond the little rules that order stone,
farmers, or the fan of delta soil.

Seek not, my soul, the life of the immortals.
Even among the very smallest rills and

broadest river basins,
logarithmic proportions hold
between stream order and the length of streams
of given lesser order, and between
stream order and the multitude of streamlets.
Rivers most resemble trees,

Not just as schema, but as organism:
parts arranged dynamically in
causal, mutual self-regulation.
Given possible discharge and prevailing
channel characters, a graded stream
is delicately adjusted to provide
the one precise velocity required for
transport of the load.

Thus rivers freely flow
according to the principle of least work,
that, like the *Odes* of Pindar, gently governs
spirit wound in matter's labyrinth.
So the river-snake's a tree,
tree a form of systematic thought,
thought, like us, an asymmetrical,
branched mirror of God.

This poem is indebted to the article "Rivers" by Luna B. Leopold.
The lines in italics are from Pindar's *Odes.*

PATTIANN ROGERS

The Voice of the Precambrian Sea

During the dearth and lack of those two thousand
Million years of death, one wished primarily
Just to grasp tightly, to compose, to circle,
To link and fasten skillfully, as one
Crusty grey bryozoan builds upon another,
To be *anything* particular, flexing and releasing
In controlled spasms, to make boundaries—replicating
Chains, membranes, epitheliums—to latch on with power
As hooked mussels now adhere to rocky beaches;
To roll up tightly, fistlike, as a water possum,
Spine and skin, curls against the cold;
To become godlike with transformation.

And in that time one eventually wished,
With the dull swell and fall of the surf, to rise up
Out of oneself, to move straight into the violet
Billowing of evening as a willed structure of flight
Trailing feet, or by six pins to balance
Above the shore on a swollen blue lupine, tender,
Almost sore with sap, to shimmer there,
Specific and alone, two yellow wings
Like splinters of morning.

One yearned simultaneously to be invisible,
In the way the oak toad is invisible among
The ashy debris of the scrub-forest floor;
To be grandiose as deserts are grandiose
With punctata and peccaries, Joshua tree,
Saguaro and the mule-ears blossom; to be precise
As the long gleaming hairs of the gourami, swaying
And touching, find the moss and roughage
Of the pond bottom with precision; to stitch
And stitch (that dream) slowly and exactly
As a woman at her tapestry with needle and thread

Sews each succeeding canopy of the rain forest
And with silver threads creates at last
The shining eyes of the capuchins huddled
Among the black leaves of the upper branches.

One longed to be able to taste the salt
Of pity, to hold by bones the stone of grief,
To take in by acknowledgement the light
Of spring lilies in a purple vase, five white
Birds flying before a thunderhead, to become
Infinite by reflection, announcing out loud
In one's own language, by one's own voice,
The fabrication of these desires, this day
Of their recitation.

A. R. AMMONS

Expressions of Sea Level

Peripherally the ocean
marks itself
　against the gauging land
it erodes and
builds:

it is hard to name
the changeless:
speech without words,
　silence renders it:
and mid-ocean,

sky sealed unbroken to sea,
　there is no way to know
the ocean's speech,
intervolved and markless,
breaking against

　no boulder-held fingerland:
broken, surf things are expressions:
the sea speaks far from its core,
far from its center relinquishes the
long-held roar:

of any mid-sea
speech, the yielding resistances
of wind and water, spray,
swells, whitecaps, moans,
　it is a dream the sea makes,

an inner problem, a self-deep
dark and private anguish
　revealed in small,
by hints, to
keen watchers on the shore:

only with the staid land
is the level conversation really held:
only in the meeting of rock and
    sea is
hard relevance shattered into light:

upbeach the clam shell
    holds smooth dry sand,
remembrance of tide:
water can go at
least that high: in

    the night, if you stay
to watch, or
if you come tomorrow at the right time,
you can see the shell caught
again in wash, the

sand turbulence changed,
new sand left smooth: if
the shell washes loose,
flops over,
    buries its rim in flux,

it will not be silence for
a shell that spoke: the
    half-buried back will
tell how the ocean dreamed
breakers against the land:

into the salt marshes the water comes fast with rising tide:
an inch of rise spreads by yards
    through tidal creeks, round fingerways of land:
the marsh grasses stem-logged
combine wind and water motions,
    slow from dry trembling
to heavier motions of wind translated through

cushioned stems; tide-held slant of grasses
    bent into the wind.

    is there a point of rest where
    the tide turns: is there one
    infinitely tiny higher touch
on the legs of egrets, the
skin of back, bay-eddy reeds:
    is there an instant when fullness is,
    without loss, complete: is there a
    statement perfect in its speech:

how do you know the moon
is moving: see the dry
casting of the beach worm
    dissolve at the
delicate rising touch:

that is the
    expression of sea level.
the talk of giants,
of ocean, moon, sun, of everything,
spoken in a dampened grain of sand.

Who Uses Whom

The grasses
figured it out
many winds ago: you can trust
the moving ocean of air.
So their sex
is all superficial,
just a lot of stamens
wavin' in the breeze
letting go.
Lower on the same stem
nets of stigmas
sift the genebearing
air. There's a tryst in the wind. Later
these organs
will wither, brown, the seed
oh, all for the seed,
grow. You can see the oats'
seedpods pendant,
like a school of feeding fish, then
the unobserved snap, out, the awn's
long hard awl of a point emerging
surprisingly part of the seed.
A lure is cast
on the fluid air,
fishing for ground below.
And the wind, what does it get
for all this matchmaking and delivery?
Some oxygen for its body; a spirit,
the bearable lightness of pollen;
the grasses' sough, its sole sound;
a shape for itself, lolloping madly
up slope.

TIM SEIBLES

Something Silver-White

Last night
I saw the moon
and remembered the earth
is also just a rock
riding the infinite dark
wave of space—that
somewhere else
deep down in the Milky Way
someone very different
could look up from a garden
to see something silver-white
candling faintly above a hilltop
and think *that dull star seems*
so weary near the rest, not knowing

that all of us are living
on that small taste of light
buying food, calling friends,
killing each other, sleeping,
and sometimes staring back
into the speckled blackness.
You know   you can spend
your whole life
glancing at your watch
while everything mysterious
does everything mysterious
the way gravity keeps everybody
close to the ground.

It *is* hard to believe this
huge, wet stone is always
flying through space—and hard
to admit there's really nothing
to hold onto   while we build houses

and fences and thousands of churches
as though this globe were just
a fat blossom atop some iron stalk
grown from God's belly.

After sailing this blue ark
so many years together
you might think
we would be kinder
because, no matter what
anybody says about
anybody else, we were all born
to this planet suddenly
blinking under the same star
and the evening sky
means the universe
is floating.

BRUCE BERGER

Astrophysicists

To show how planetarily trite,
How cosmically backward we are,
They say we're a junior satellite
Of a most unpropitious star,

A little platform of frustrated gazers
Quite unbrushed by the thrill
Of postmeridians blazing with quasars
Or nebulae by De Mille,

Unjammed by dust clouds, losing no gas
Down gravity's Gothic cellar,
Twin to no death star, too middle-class
To be kinkily quasi-stellar,

Unwarped by hyperspace and far
Too Republican to be
Too close to the hub or the rim of our
Pedestrian galaxy,

Paddling predictably through the slather
And spume of parochial skies
That baffle our astrophysicists' rather
American notions of size,

A very small array of ground
Roundish and airy and damp,
Commuting wearily around
Our dim suburban lamp.

That's us, then, in our designer jeans,
Inveterate Trivia players
With our little moon shots, our Sistines,
Our frivolous Himalayas,

Our rufous hummingbirds, our Trout
Quintets, our Danish beer,

Our verse so bad no cosmonaut
Would think to look for life here,

Shriveling every frontal lobe
That hauls itself back from fat
Falstaffian space to find our globe
So relatively flat,

Our airspace ever more licensed and vocal,
Our bottomland ever compacter,
Our vanishing phyla plugged to the local
Hydrogen reactor—

It makes the astrophysicist nod
Who has heard the novae sing,
This third rate star with the very odd
Star sapphire on its third ring.

BILLY COLLINS

Earthling

You have probably come across
those scales in planetariums
that tell you how much you
would weigh on other planets.

You have noticed the fat ones
lingering on the Mars scale
and the emaciated slowing up
the line for Neptune.

As a creature of average weight,
I fail to see the attraction.

Imagine squatting in the wasteland
of Pluto, all five tons of you,
or wandering around Mercury
wondering what to do next with your ounce.

How much better to step onto
the simple bathroom scale,
a happy earthling feeling
the familiar ropes of gravity,

157 pounds standing soaking wet
a respectful distance from the sun.

On Earth

Any sun that comes, even
one not ours, could have these lakes
to drink out of, any time.

And other laws could come besides
the ones we have, all springing
from a force that makes them right.

The lives we have, while we have them,
can measure time, before and after
today, to use or give away.

On earth it is like this, a strange
gift we hold, while we look around.

CARL DENNIS

The Anthropic Cosmological Principle

Maybe the new theory is true, and the odds
For intelligent life beyond our planet
Are as slim as they were here,
And the only voices ever to reach us
From beyond will be our children's,
Our earth in a thousand years the mother of colonies
On planets never before inhabited.

Long after the sun swells in its final flare
To consume our world, they'll remember us
Just as immigrants here remember the old country in stories.
The Earth will sound to them like a garden,
More a land of myth than of history,
Its green valleys and blue skies incredible,
The way its grasses climbed the hills untended,
The way its birds alighted in groves nobody planted
To trill phrases nobody taught them.

A house like this one, on a street like mine,
Will be a house from a dim, heroic age
When their own fate was decided. Just as I stay up late
To study a narrative of the Civil War
And marvel how close the country came to dissolving,
The great experiment cancelled, the slaves still slaves,
So they will marvel as they study our hostilities
How close we came to spoiling their chances,
Their galactic cities bombed into fictions, their farms,
Schools, churches, opera houses, and union halls
Sponged from the blackboard with the crowds
Cheering on the dock on Regatta Day.

Are they real or not? That's the question
That has them worried. Are they waiting on a road
Reachable from the starting point of today?
Impossible to imagine how remote I'd feel

After rummaging in a trunk all afternoon,
Searching for proof that I paid my taxes,
If I found a letter proving I was never born,
That the mother who might have been mine
Ran off on her wedding day and was never heard from,
That I'm only my would-be father's fantasy
As he lies in his empty house on his deathbed
Dreaming of the life he might have lived.

Today I seem to be real as I stop for groceries.
I may be moody returning to the empty house
I promised myself to fill, but not so lonely
If I think of the distant, stellar observers.
What voices deeper than reason and will
I've failed to hear isn't so hard a question
As why I've been fated to decide their destiny.
And what's my strategy for the day, they wonder,
To prompt them to practice songs of joy,
Not dirges?

7

Animal

It is wonderful how things work . . .

A. R. AMMONS

PATTIANN ROGERS

The Rites of Passage

The inner cell of each frog egg laid today
In these still open waters is surrounded
By melanin pigment, by a jelly capsule
Acting as cushion to the falling of the surf,
As buffer to the loud crow-calling
Coming from the cleared forests to the north.

At 77° the single cell cleaves in 90 minutes,
Then cleaves again and in five hours forms the hollow
Ball of the blastula. In the dark, 18 hours later,
Even as a shuffle in the grass moves the shadows
On the shore and the stripes of the moon on the sand
Disappear and the sounds of the heron jerk
Across the lake, the growing blastula turns itself
Inside out unassisted and becomes a gut.

What is the source of the tension instigating next
The rudimentary tail and gills, the cobweb of veins?
What is the impetus slowly directing the hard-core
Current right up the scale to that one definite moment
When a fold of cells quivers suddenly for the first time
And someone says loudly "heart," born, beating steadily,
Bearing now in the white water of the moon
The instantaneous distinction of being liable to death?

Above me, the full moon, round and floating deep
In its capsule of sky, never trembles.
In ten thousand years it will never involute
Its white frozen blastula to form a gut,
Will never by a heart be called born.

Think of that part of me wishing tonight to remember
The split-second edge before the beginning,
To remember by a sudden white involution of sight,

By a vision of tension folding itself
Inside clear open waters, by imitating a manipulation
Of cells in a moment of distinction, wishing to remember
The entire language made during that crossing.

KERRY JOHANSSEN

The 9+2 Roseate Anatomy of Microtubules

Nature is Imagination.
William Blake

It would be like drawing with a stick
nine circles in a circle in the snow,

with two more centered inside
the ring, and imagining them all

extending, down into the earth
and up through sky, as seemingly

discrete cylinders, flexing alive
in lung cilia and flagellating sperm,

empowered by our meticulous
mitochrondrial cells.

It could be like tracing nine
orbs in a hoop in snow, two

within, and all sturdy as the oaks
buried upright under buildings in Chicago

before our wars and the wind began
decorating winter trees by the lake

with plastic shreds as majestic bronze
mares and stallions rear their heads.

It might be like sketching with a twig
the smallest possible flower,

as whales veer around floating continents
and moons ellipse planets ellipsing the sun.

Sea Lilies

aren't any kind of flower,
but we fancy they flaunt calyx,
petiole, and sepal, imagine
them feeding ocean bees,
pretend their chalk-stems
bear sap, their splayed feet,
clasping against the currents,
are real roots.

We call them lilies,
these beasts in drag
that wave petal-arms
in the wind of the seabed.
Having no scent, no innocence
or grace, they sense only
where's my next bite,
measure time in food-gulps.

Sea lilies scatter their young
like pollen before their bones
become stone mirrors;
they carry the ages
lightly in the hollow stalks,
spread their corollas to eat
the passing moments,
finding no need to bloom.

A. R. AMMONS

Mechanism

Honor a going thing, goldfinch, corporation, tree,
      morality: any working order,
    animate or inanimate: it

has managed directed balance,
      the incoming and outgoing energies are working right,
    some energy left to the mechanism,

some ash, enough energy held
      to maintain the order in repair,
    assure further consumption of entropy,

expending energy to strengthen order:
      honor the persisting reactor,
    the container of change, the moderator: the yellow

bird flashes black wing-bars
      in the new-leaving wild cherry bushes by the bay,
    startles the hawk with beauty,

flitting to a branch where
      flash vanishes into stillness,
    hawk addled by the sudden loss of sight:

honor the chemistries, platelets, hemoglobin kinetics,
      the light-sensitive iris, the enzymic intricacies
    of control,

the gastric transformations, seed
      dissolved to acrid liquors, synthesized into
    chirp, vitreous humor, knowledge,

blood compulsion, instinct: honor the
      unique genes,
    molecules that reproduce themselves, divide into

sets, the nucleic grain transmitted
      in slow change through ages of rising and falling form,
    some cells set aside for the special work, mind

or perception rising into orders of courtship,
      territorial rights, mind rising
    from the physical chemistries

to guarantee that genes will be exchanged, male
      and female met, the satisfactions cloaking a deeper
    racial satisfaction:

heat kept by a feathered skin:
      the living alembic, body heat maintained (bunsen
    burner under the flask)

so the chemistries can proceed, reaction rates
      interdependent, self-adjusting, with optimum
    efficiency—the vessel firm, the flame

staying: isolated, contained reactions! the precise and
      necessary worked out of random, reproducible,
    the handiwork redeemed from chance, while the

goldfinch, unconscious of the billion operations
      that stay its form, flashes, chirping (not a
    great songster) in the bay cherry bushes wild of leaf.

A. R. AMMONS

Identity

    1)   An individual spider web
        identifies a species:

an order of instinct prevails
    through all accidents of circumstance,
       though possibility is
high along the peripheries of
spider
        webs:
        you can go all
   around the fringing attachments

   and find
disorder ripe,
entropy rich, high levels of random,
   numerous occasions of accident:

    2)   the possible settings
       of a web are infinite:

how does
the spider keep
    identity
while creating the web
in a particular place?

   how and to what extent
    and by what modes of chemistry
    and control?

it is
wonderful
   how things work: I will tell you
    about it
    because

it is interesting
and because whatever is
moves in weeds
 and stars and spider webs
and known
    is loved:
  in that love,
  each of us knowing it,
  I love you,

for it moves within and beyond us,
   sizzles in
winter grasses, darts and hangs with bumblebees
by summer windowsills:

   I will show you
the underlying that takes no image to itself,
   cannot be shown or said,
but weaves in and out of moons and bladderweeds,
   is all and
  beyond destruction
  because created fully in no
particular form:

   if the web were perfectly pre-set,
   the spider could
  never find
  a perfect place to set it in: and

   if the web were
perfectly adaptable,
if freedom and possibility were without limit,
   the web would
lose its special identity:

  the row-strung garden web
keeps order at the center
where space is freest (interesting that the freest

          "medium" should
          accept the firmest order)

and that
order
                    diminishes toward the
periphery
          allowing at the points of contact
                    entropy equal to entropy.

Genetic Sequence

A caterpillar spits out a sac of silk
where it lies entombed while its genes
switch on and off like lights
on a pinball machine. If every cell
contains the entire sequence
constituting what or who the creature is,
how does a certain clump of cells
know to line up side by side
and turn into wings, then shut off
while another clump blinks on
spilling pigment into the creature's
emerald green blood, waves of color
flowing into wingscales—black, orange,
white—each zone receptive only to the color
it's destined to become. And then
the wings unfold, still wet from their making,
and for a dangerous moment hold steady
while they stiffen and dry, the double-
layered wing a protolanguage—one side
warning enemies, the other luring mates.
And then the pattern-making cells go dormant,
and the butterfly has mastered flight.

Essay on Intelligence: One

The female digger wasp
maintains several burrows
for developing offspring.
As the day begins, she visits
and inspects each tunnel
determining which contain
eggs requiring no food,
which contain larvae
needing two or three
caterpillars to eat, and which
the pupated offspring sealed
in for metamorphosis. On
the basis of her inspection,
the wasp knows how much
prey to capture and where
to deliver the food. If the
occupants of burrows
are switched in the night,
the mother adjusts to the change,
stocking each nursery
according to its need. But if
the offspring are switched
after her inspection,
she will spend the day
stocking with caterpillars
a burrow containing eggs
and will seal off young larvae
to starve. She will touch
and examine an egg many times
without realizing it needs no food.

Essay on Intelligence: Two

Language has been the central
event in human evolution.
Simple emotional utterances
evoked in sex, anger, and fear
activate the primitive area
near the *corpus callosum*,
that ribbon tying together
the hemispheres. No one knows
how our ancestors got beyond
the scream, grunt, and moan
to string meaningless phonemes
together until the sounds
meant something in tandem
they didn't mean alone.
The brain area critical to
complex language processing
is located above the left ear
in men, but appears to be
more diffuse in women.
By borrowing the mental
structures for syntax
to judge combinations of
possible actions, our species
has extended its intelligence,
foresight being an essential
element of that faculty.
We do this by talking silently
to ourselves, making narratives
out of what might happen next and then
applying syntaxlike rules of
combination to rate a scenario
as dangerous nonsense, mere nonsense,

possible, likely, or logical.
This allows a hypothesis
to die in our stead.
Unlike animals that respond
more impulsively to a stimulus,
our continual adjustment of
internal to external relations
opens the way for postponing
action, deliberating, reflection—
a new quality of mind evolving,
which, quite naturally, feels
confused by its urgencies,
because the ancient part
wants to act and the newer part
insists on imagining action.

after William H. Calvin, Herbert Spencer, Karl Popper

Essay on Intelligence: Three

After many years of language training
in the Yerkes Primate Lab *(our animals
have indoor/outdoor access and may
withdraw from lessons at will)* Sherman
the chimp, after correctly categorizing

> socket wrench
> stick
> banana
> bread
> key
> money
> orange

as either food or tool,
used the incorrect lexigram
to classify a sponge.

The chimp has one hundred keys
to choose from. First, he was
asked to sort food and tools
into two bins. Later,
instead of bins, to press
the lexigram for food or tool.

He could string lexigrams to say

> please
> machine
> give
> piece
> of banana

Sherman's apparent mistake
was subsequently read
as the interpreter's

misunderstanding of the animal's
intent. An active eater,
Sherman is prone to
sucking liquids from a sponge,
often chewing and swallowing
the tool as if it were food.

ALISON HAWTHORNE DEMING

Essay on Intelligence: Four

The male satin bowerbird builds a woven platform ten feet square, supporting an avenue of woven sticks, walls a foot high arching over the floor, decked with bits of colored shell, fruit, seedheads. He shows a preference for objects green and blue, for blossoms uncommon in the local environment. Perishable decorations such as flowers are replaced. Some bowers are painted either blue, black, or green, using a wad of bark as a paint brush and crushed fruit, charcoal, or blue laundry powder as paint. The male tries to entice females into his bower by picking up in his bill a flower or snail shell, posturing, displaying, and dancing. He gives a whirring call while fluffing up his feathers and flapping his wings to the beat of his vocalizations. Mating is often so violent that the bower is wrecked, and the exhausted female can scarcely crawl away. When a courted female is won over and starts to solicit copulation, the male often changes his mind and chases her away. Thus a female may have to make many visits to a bower before she overcomes her fear. After mating, the female constructs a nest at least 200 yards from the bower and bears sole responsibility for feeding the young.

Variant objects displayed in bowers: moss, beetle heads, acorns, cellophane, brown stones, blue glass, red leaves, poker chips (like colors stacked), red fruits, blue feathers, black and orange bracket fungi, butterflies.

Essay on Intelligence: Five

Unfold the cortex and lay it
on the table—it's thin and smooth
as a napkin, as in an embryo
until as the animal grows
the tissue begins to ripple and
crush so that the neural tangle
will fit inside the skull.
The number of folds, how deeply
crenellated, and the direction
in which the tissue is pressed
vary dramatically from animal to animal.
To count the neural connections
in the human brain, one per second,
would take thirty-two million years.
How is it then that "I" am one thing,
my life as dear to me as if I knew
each neural pathway by heart?
That jungle, lush and interwoven,
a brief protected habitat
that writes the rules for its survival
in a language I can't read, but must believe.

   after Gerald Edelman

Essay on Intelligence: Six

Inasmuch as awareness is a process
carried out by the central nervous system,
neuroscientists gather data from brains
engaged in complex tasks. Electrical potentials
accompany the pulse of neurons and the modulating
synaptical hum.

          The most prominent potentials
are alpha waves, evident when the human subject
lies quietly, eyes closed, not engaged in any
particular mental task. If asked to solve
a math problem, the subject's alpha waves
diminish and merge into irregular
noisy signals.

        In the "oddball"
experiment the subject hears eighty words
that rhyme with *cake* and twenty that do not,
eight hundred times *Harold* and two hundred
Maude—patterns of repetition
that set an expectation in the mind.
The rare stimuli (omission of the expected)
elicit the largest P300 waves
indicating that according to the brain
(its attraction to novelty and meaning)
something important is going on.

         My P300s
must be hopping now because my new
Glaswegian friend, to egg on my writing,
just left a chocolate bar outside my door—
Cadbury's Dairy Milk Wildlife Bar—the wrapper
decked with watercolored monarch butterflies,
a brief ecological message, and inside,

the candy, each segment, embossed
with leopard, fawn, or penguin, the priests of marketing
having had a vision that eating chocolate
could help us save the wild: *Eat this in remembrance of me.*

Essay on Intelligence: Seven

The broken-wing display of a plover
involves awkward flapping
that resembles actual injury.
Such behavior draws a predator's
attention away from a nest.
Some researchers, obeying
the Law of Parsimony, describe
the display as a hysterical response
made by a bird convulsed
between parental drives and
the tendency to flee or attack.
"I'm helpless" is their reading
of the plover's dance. Others
consider the display a haphazard reflex
switching on when the bird is
"in a hormonal condition" and
in the presence of a moving object.
Most researchers resist attributing
to the plover first-order intentionality—
"the bird wants to lead the intruder
away from the young." Why do they
seem to want to disprove
the possibility that animals
can think? Perhaps (to take
the generous view) they don't want
to become one of history's
mistakes, another example of
human blindness, our celebrated
ability to see what we want,
rather than what's there.
Consider the fate of George Romanes,
Darwin's disciple, whose 1884 work,
Animal Intelligence, addressed

the continuity of mental faculties
among creatures, citing the example of
Icelandic mice said to have been observed
storing supplies of berries
inside dried mushrooms, loading the rations
onto dried cow-droppings, then
launching their supply ships and
sailing them across rivers
using their tails as rudders.

Os

Once the bone that holds the incisors
of vertebrates was believed, in absentia,
to be the key to human language:
the anatomical Rubicon line of our caste.

When it was found, at home in our talkative jaw,
holding our canines same as a garter snake's tooth,
that ur-morphologist sent a bucking-up letter.
Said Goethe, to the mildly and deeply dismayed

"Something that gives me boundless pleasure . . .
the *os intermaxillare* in man has been found.
It is not missing; it is there too!
It should please you greatly as well."

What *so* high joy in an animal *os*?
Only this: at the bone we speak of continuum
and the door of creation is open:
so atmosphere and earth beget their love

in bursting renewals of cumulus hills,
in long suffering gussets and roots,
so simile noses in ruminant gentleness,
sound as a dollar, blind as a bat.

ALBERT GOLDBARTH

Tarpan and Aurochs

> In certain cases, it is possible to recreate extinct animals through careful
> breeding of present-day species. Two species that have been successfully
> recreated are a type of wild horse and a prototypical form of cattle.
>   The World Almanac Book of the Strange #2

Eventually you'll be called. It will be
over water, or will appear to be
over a great expanse of water, no matter
where you are: the passage will be dark
with just a far, red rind of light that seems
to say an unseen shore. It may not be
a "shore," but water comes to mind, and
fish: some matrix-you, an early time of day
or life: a place that's amniotic. There's something calling
—your name, you think. And you hear it as if
over water. It will happen, and it will happen to you
in just this way. —Your real name, who you were
all along. Hoof-in-the-walking, Horn-from-the-skull,
Small-chain-of-original-protein.

*   *   *

In the subway car, peripheral vision flickers
unexpectedly with the B-train on the next track over
starting up, so giving you that second's (or less) illusion of
backwards travel. Travel backwards,
then: a blurred face in a length of A-train
rewound like a film. Who hasn't once
seen skydivers rise like that, the 'chutes above them
closing like flowers photography's run wrongway, then finally
folding like flowers, compactly back into the seed
—and not imagined himself in the car that tunnels
retrograde through time, to be the string
of metabolic process not yet even hard-wired

into the neural circuits, not yet even fetal REM, for which
midwifery hands are so macroscopic they don't exist.

*　　*　　*

There are paintings in which the souls of men are
breaking out of their bodies and rising like steam
from warm, torn bread, like steam with a very
calm face—and you see the painters really
believed in this, along with gold and rats
it's what the Middle Ages was all about.
The point of view is almost that of the souls'
—the flesh we take for granted, so everything paint
can mean to semblance is given to spirit's
verisimilitude. Finally, looking long enough,
the opposite occurs: it's the bodies of men we need
convincing of　did we really belong
to those things on the ground? (A waft, a spark,
is enough now.) Could such rough husks be ancestral?

*　　*　　*

I said *fetal REM*. The friend of a friend has found
the migratory stopping-place for North America's
monarchs: in the mountains north of Mexico City
37,000,000 drowse in conifers, one dun molecule or two of
thorax-susurration away from not being
anything at all. After sex, a lady asks
how many butterflies one of our heartbeats
could power. I turn to her not even knowing
the width of the border between a man and a woman
—slickness atoms-thick? or something so
large as prehistory and we'll never cross it
in this life? That the fetus's eyelids correspond
to one of those idling butterflies, I know, the way
we all know the travel of light though perhaps not its formula.

*　　*　　*

There's no measure for that distance. —But
you. Eventually you'll be called; you'll go, and be
a standard unit through incredible space. No
I don't want to turn from the pleasures of mattress,
glass, the well-bound book, the well-glazed duck
l'orange with almond slivers, electrical pylon
softened in morning snow, the nylon bunched about
her toes then straightened transparently over a thigh . . .
But we'll be called, so must prepare; must even
understand our hands on rocks, in sun, regress
to lizards; even learn to love the light the way the nuclei
of algae do, entire; even learn to love the dust and
even the subatomic bones of the dust; and make
the tarpan and aurochs, name them, know them eye to eye.

8
Human

Propounding new solutions to the riddle of the sphinx . . .

HOWARD NEMEROV

PATTIANN ROGERS

The Origin of Order

Stellar dust has settled.
It is green underwater now in the leaves
Of the yellow crowfoot. Its potentialities
Are gathered together under pine litter
As emerging flower of the pink arbutus.
It has gained the power to make itself again
In the bone-filled egg of osprey and teal.

One could say this toothpick grasshopper
Is a cloud of decayed nebula congealed and perching
On his female mating. The tortoise beetle,
Leaving the stripped veins of morning-glory vines
Like licked bones, is a straw-colored swirl
Of clever gases.

At this moment there are dead stars seeing
Themselves as marsh and forest in the eyes
Of muskrat and shrew, disintegrated suns
Making songs all night long in the throats
Of crawfish frogs, in the rubbings and gratings
Of the red-legged locust. There are spirits of orbiting
Rock in the shells of pointed winkles
And apple snails, ghosts of extinct comets caught
In the leap of darting hare and bobcat, revolutions
Of rushing stone contained in the sound of these words.

Maybe the paths of the Pleiades and Coma clusters
Have been compelled to mathematics by the mind
Contemplating the nature of itself
In the motions of stars. The pattern
of the starry summer night might be identical
To the structure of the summer heavens circling
Inside the skull. I can feel time speeding now

In all directions deeper and deeper into the black oblivion
Of the electrons directly behind my eyes.

Child of the sky, ancestor of the sky, the mind
Has been obligated from the beginning
To create an ordered universe
As the only possible proof
Of its own inheritance.

CHARLES HARPER WEBB

Descent

FOR MY SON

Let
there be
amino acids,
and there were: a slop
of molecules in ancient seas,
building cell walls to keep their
distance, dividing, replicating, starting
to diversify, one growing oars, one rotors, one
a wiry tail, lumping into clusters—cyanobacteria, sea-
worms, medusae, trilobites, lobe-finned fish dragging onto
land, becoming thrinaxodon, protoceratops, growing larger—
diplodocus, gorgosaurus—dying out—apatosaurus, tyrannosaurus—
mammals evolving from shrew-like deltatheridium into hyenadon, eohippus,
mammoth, saber-tooth, dire wolf, australopithecus rising on two feet, homo erectus
tramping from Africa into Europe and Asia, thriving like a weed that will grow anywhere—
jungle, desert, snow-pack—the genetic rivers flowing downhill now: a husband's skull crushed
in the Alps, a Tartar raping a green-eyed girl who dies in childbirth, whose daughter falls in
love with a Viking who takes her to Istanbul, a Celt who marries a Saxon, a weaver
who abducts the daughter of a witch, a son who steals his father's gold, a girl
who loses one eye leaping from a tree, dozens who die of smallpox,
cholera, black plague, a knight, a prostitute, thieves, carpenters,
farmers, poachers, blacksmiths, seamstresses, peddlers of
odds and ends, an Irishman who sells his family into
servitude, a Limey who jumps ship in New York,
Jews who flee Hungary, a midwife, an X-ray
machine repairman, a psychologist,
a writer, all flowing down,
converging on the great
delta, the point
of all this:
you.

Evolution

Now the statistics are in, we can see
How unconvincing our story is,
Packed with too many hairbreadth escapes,
Too many changes in climate at the final moment.
Dust clouds from a passing shower of meteors
Deadly to plants required by our competition
But not by us. Nothing here for a reader
Who expects a plot to be probable.

The reef pushes up and blocks the inlet,
And the new-made lake silts into marsh,
Choking the fish that adapted over eons
To life in open water, to storms and sharks.
But the freakish lungfish, slow and clumsy,
Cakes itself in mud and dozes through the dry spell.
The flood that sweeps the lowlands
Drowns the burrowers, sober and industrious,
While the one drunk, snuggled in a hollow log
And snoring, is lifted up.
He bobs along on his one-man ark.
He bumps awake next morning on a mountain,
Yawns, rubs his eyes, and gapes.
Our father, who vows never to drink again near bedtime.
So much for proof the fit win out.

This photo of Dad and his boys
Wading in Shadrack Creek Sunday before last
To fish for salmon can be no more real
Than the fairy tale about salmon
Wasting their strength flailing up the rapids.
Might as well credit the fitness of sister eel
Crawling without hands and knees from wells to rivers,
Swimming without a map to the far Sargasso

To join the mating dance of mermaids and mermen
If the sea happens to be calm enough.

No power that claims to be practical
Would choose to embody itself like this in history.
And yet with a little effort we can work up something
To prove how likely it all is,
How suited we are to the sandy soil we spring from,
To clay or loam, marshy or dry.

DENISE DUHAMEL

The Future of Vaginas and Penises

Descendants of Darwin predict a longer penis
as time goes on, as surely as our foreheads will expand
and our bodies will shed their needless hair.
In each generation, the vagina will tilt a miniscule angle
so our greatest of great granddaughters
will know the most pleasurable of unhurried sex acts.
Can't picture the millennial-slow realignment of the vagina?
Imagine then, if you will, the blade of your windshield wiper
traveling an arc in slow motion, forward but not back.
A caveman, with his penis stub, rushed
in and out, probably entering a cavewoman from behind.
But as he extended, she shifted her insides
until finally we, and some of the others, like gorillas,
could savor intercourse, face to face.
This brings us to the puzzle of the clitoris.
Is genital evolution only about successful propagation?
What about a woman's orgasm?
Will her clitoris grow to be many more pink inches?
Will it migrate down towards the vaginal opening
for easier penile stimulation? Will the vulva swell
and double its number of folds? Future men
and women, so sexually happy, will lose their need
for war and divorce. Bald lovers will cuddle
by the timeless fire, their hairless bodies as naked
as skinned animals. Vulnerable, men and women
will honeymoon on the Galapagos Islands, enjoying
their smooth erotic lives, paying tribute to generations
of awkward groping partners before them.

ALICE JONES

The Cell

Like every reception, there's food
    and dancing and bumping
        into all those quirky

relatives: blood, Great-Aunt Henriette
    says, is thicker than
        anything, it's in

the genes, she says, as if she just
    discovered the cell,
        the body's time capsule,

recording history for the clumsy, naked
    bipeds who hover at
        the edge of fire,

evolving into creatures who learn
    the cells workings:
        how it sucks up

water from the surrounding matrix
    through sticky-lipped
        pores; how each tiny

apparatus for food or sex floats
    in this one drop of opaque
        saline—the primal jelly;

how it transcribes proteins from
    inborn templates for the
        generations of identical daughters;

how it prepares for the wedding, swollen
    chromosomes unwind, line up,
        pull to the center and

disperse in their Virginia Reel,
    mitosis: then the cleaving in two,
        the rift, the birth, transformed.

ALICE JONES

The Blood

The gift, prepared in humid kitchens
of hematopoietic marrow, is packed
into red cells, the sticky biconcave discs
mixed in with everything—plasma, monocytes,
platelets, polymorphonuclear leukocytes,
lymphs, proteins, fibrin ready to repair
any leaks or tears—all go coursing out
the arch of great vessels, through the large
bore pipes, the wash of tides, not moon-driven
like those of the globe but heart-felt, the force
of the meat-pump pulsing through 60,000 miles
of vessels, propels the concoction down huge tubes
to small sustaining arteries, to unnamed branches,
then capillaries, through their fenestrated pores
the host of red corpuscles marches out, to deliver
the bound molecule of oxygen—a communion—
then transport CO_2, through valved, passive veins,
back to the body's airy waste bin to exhale,
burgundy shifts to crimson in the cycle—
right heart, lungs, left heart, then back down
the grand aortic arch to each beefy muscle
as myosin demands; they imagined the body
to be, not a map of spillways, not an urban
plumbing system, but an ocean, which,
when the closed circulation was first described,
vanished into the invisible realm of the cell,
where salt tides ebb and flow, gated
by the membrane's channels, the tiny sea
of each walled compartment takes in
everything by drops: mouth-fed babies, calling
for more, the blood brings succor to each.

ALICE JONES

The Inner Ear

A lost sea animal,
some shrunken nautilus,
must have wandered down
this waxy tunnel
seeking refuge from
the noisy world,
to hide behind a glassy
oval window, a plate-
like shell, protection
for the quivering
creature, sensitive
to each vibration,
to every change in pitch.

Gravity-keepers, three
semicircular canals,
our internal gyroscope,
respond to any element
of tilt, so the saccule
and utricle always know
where earth is, like
a toddler ever-conscious
of her mother's presence;
within the bony labyrinth,
the otoliths send signals,
and we decide to root our
feet or hold on tight.

The snail-like cochlea
holds everything in whorls,
the spiral organs swim
in moving cortilymph,
ossicles tap the tympanum,
hammer-tuned hair cells

respond, transmit their
pitched reverberations
through that bony bell,
the skull, creating
clamorous harmonics,
neuronal melodies,
corporeal music.

ALICE JONES

The Larynx

Under the epiglottic flap
the long-ringed tube sinks
its shaft down to the bronchial
fork, divides from two
to four then infinite branches,
each ending finally in a clump
of transparent sacs knit
with small vessels into a mesh
that sponge-like soaks up breath
and gives it off with a push
from the diaphragm's muscular wall,
forces wind out of the lungs'
wide tree, up through this organ's
single pipe, through the puzzle
box of gristle, where resonant
plates of cartilage fold
into shield, horns, bows,
bound by odd half-spirals
of muscles that modulate air
as it rises through this empty place
at our core, where lip-like
folds stretch across the vestibule,
small and tough, they flutter,
bend like birds' wings finding
just the right angle to stay
airborne; here the cords arch
in the hollow of this ancient instrument,
curve and vibrate to make song.

The Lungs

In the tidal flux, the lobed pair avidly
    grasp the invisible.

Along oblique fissures, gnarled vascular roots
    anchor the puffed cushions,

soot-mottled froth, the pink segmented sponges
    that soak up the atmosphere,

then squeezed by the rising dome of the diaphragm's
    muscular bellows, exhale.

Braids of vessels and cartilage descend
    in vanishing smallness,

to grape clusters of alveoli, the sheerest
    of membranes, where oxygen

crosses the infinite cellular web, where air turns
    to blood, spirit to flesh,

in a molecular transubstantiation, to bring rich
    food to that red engine,

the heart, which like an equitable mother, pumps
    to each organ and appendage

according to need, so even the cells in the darkest
    corners can breathe.

Beam 4

The human eye, a sphere of waters and tissue, absorbs an energy that has come ninety-three million miles from another sphere, the sun. The eye may be said to be sun in other form.

It is part of a spectrum of receptors, and if we could only 'see' more widely the night sky would be 'brighter' than the moon. Matter smaller than the shortest wavelength of light cannot be seen.

Pressure on the surface of an eye makes vision, though what these same pressures focus to the radial inwardness of a dragonfly in flight is unimaginable. Through pressure also, the head-over-heals is crossed right-side-up, in eye as camera. (It is possible to take a cow's eyeball and thin the rear wall of it with a knife, fit it front forward in a tube, and the tube pointed at an elm will image an upside down elm.)

The front of the eye is a convex glass, alive, and light bent through its curve strikes a lens. This lens is behind an iris—pushing it into the shape of a volcano. In light, the iris appears as a rayed core of color, its center hole dilating dark to day, transformed instantly into what man's twinned inner hemispheres call sight.

The retina is its bowl-shaped back—the cones at retinal center growing through intersections with rods, toward rods at the rim. Through this mesh, ray seizes ray to see. In the rods there is a two-part molecule that is unlinked by light. One quantum of light unlinks one molecule, and five rods are needed to perceive the difference. Some stars are at this threshold, and can only be seen by the sides of the eyes. The eye can see a wire .01 inch in diameter at a distance of 100 yards. The retina itself seeks equilibrium.

Though to look at the sun directly causes blindness, sight is an intricately precise tip of branched energy that has made it possible to measure the charge of solar storm, or to calculate nova. It is possible that all universe is of a similar form.

Our eyes are blue for the same reason sky is, a scattering of reflectors: human eyes have only brown pigment.

In the embryo two stalks push from the brain, through a series of infoldings, to form optic cups. Where the optic cup reaches surface, the surface turns in and proliferates in the shape of an ingrowing mushroom. The last nerve cells to form are those farthest from light.

If I sit at my table and look at the shaft of light which enters a glass filled with water—and exits rainbow—then move my head to the left, the shaft and glass move right, and the window behind them, left. If I stand up and step to the table, the glass at its edge moves downward, while the far end of the table, and the window with it, rise straight up in the air.

No one knows the first man to stare long at a waterfall, then shift his gaze to the cliff face at its side, to find the rocks at once flow upward. But we have always known the eye to be unsleeping, and that all men are lidless Visionaries through the night. Mind & Eye are a logarithmic spiral coiled from periphery. This is called a 'spiral sweep'— a biological form which combines (as do galaxies) economy with beauty. (We define 'beauty' from symmetrical perceptions): *subjects observing a flickered pulsation of light have seen something like a Catherine-wheel reversing rotation, with a center of fine detail.* Men have found cells sensitive to light in the hearts of snails.

The human lens grows flatter for looking across a prairie, and the sparrow is able to see the seed beneath its bill—and in the same instant the hawk descending. A cat watches the-sparrow-at-the-end-of-the-world in a furred luminosity of infra-reds, enormous purples.

After a long time of light, there began to be eyes, and light began looking with itself. At the exact moment of death the pupils open full width.

RONALD JOHNSON

Beam 7

Sound is sea: pattern lapping pattern. If we erase the air and slow the sound of a struck tuning-fork in it, it would make two sets of waves interlocking the invisibility in opposite directions.

As the prong of the fork moved one way, it compressed the air at its front, which layer in turn relieves its compression by expanding the layer in front, and so back to back. As it started the other direction it left the air in front (opposite) immediately rarefied. The air beyond this expands to the rarefaction—itself becoming rarefied—forth and forth.

Compression rarefaction compression rarefaction: these alternate equidistant forces travel at the rate of 1,180 feet per second through the elasticity of air, four times that through water (whale to singing whale), and fifteen times as fast through pure steel. Men have put ear to earth to hear in advance of air.

Pattern laps pattern, and as they joined, Charles Ives heard the 19th Century in one ear, and the 20th out the other, then commenced to make a single music of them. The final chord of the 2nd Symphony is a reveille of all notes at once, his The Fourth of July ends with a fireworks of thirteen rhythmic patterns zigzagging through the winds and brasses, seven percussion lines criss-crossing these, the strings divided in twenty-fours going up and down every-which-way—and all in FFFF.

Both tuning fork and Fourth are heard by perturbations of molecules, through ever more subtle stumbling blocks, in spiral richochet, to charged branches treeing a brain.

The outer earshell leads to a membrane drum—and what pressure needed to sound this drum is equal to the intensity of light and heat received from a 50 watt electric bulb at the distance of 3,000 miles in empty space. (Though sound cannot travel, as light, through the void.) At the threshold of hearing the eardrum may be misplaced as little as a diameter of the smallest atom, hydrogen.

This starts a 'hammer' to strike an 'anvil' which nudges a 'stirrup'—all, bones—against a drum known as The Oval Window. Shut to air, this window vibrates another windowed membrane, tuning a compressed fluid between. *Here, also, is couched our sense of the vertical.*

A resonance is set up in a spiral shell-shaped receptor turned with yet another, also spiral, membrane. This is the pith of labyrinth, and as sound waves themselves it trembles two directions at once, crosswise and lengthwise.

The mind begins early to select from the buzz and humdrum, till most men end hearing nothing, when the earth speaks, but their own voices. Henry David Thoreau seems to have been the first man to re-learn to hear that *Moto Perpetuo* of the actual: the Greeks strung their lyre to the planets, but Thoreau heard his stretched from first dark sparrow to last dog baying moon.

While a bat uses its ears to see, its optics overtones, the fly hears only in frequencies of its own (and other) fly-wings. I know the housefinch singing outside the window just now heard its own song with slower and lower ear than mine, but I do not know what this means, or how it rings in finchskull. (Though all animals have an auditory range which includes hearing what they can eat, and what can eat them.)

A man once set out to see birds, but found instead he'd learned to listen: an ear better unwinds the simultaneous warblers in a summer birchwood. There, he came upon an Orpheus, all marble, holding a spiral shell to the ear of his Euridice. Turning the other way, he saw Orpheus again, listening to harmonics of midges in sun, the meadow like nightingale around him. Cat's purr, moth-wing.

The physicists tell us that all sounding bodies are in a state of stationary vibration, and that when the word *syzygy* last shook atoms, its boundary was an ever slighter pulse of heat, and hesitation of heat. Matter delights in music, and became Bach. Its dreams are the abyss and empyrean, and to that end, may move, in time, the stones themselves to sing.

Liver

Largest gland in the human body, three-pounds-plus of spongy red-
    brown meat
Shaped like a slug or a fat, finless seal lodged in the abdomen's upper
    right quadrant,
Canopied by diaphragm, nudging stomach and guts—you taste so foul
    when cooked,
So musty and rotten, who would guess that you provide protein, vitamins
    A, D, E, and B-complex,
Copper and iron? Who would guess the wealth of your accomplishments:
    blood-filter,
Storehouse for energy, aid to digestion, producer of proteins and antibodies,
    self-regenerator.
Doctors took out three-fourths of my friend Ken's liver in Germany, but
    it grew back.
Surgeons routinely take a chunk from an adult's liver and transplant it
    to a child.
The adult's liver grows back to its full size; the child's new liver grows
    as the child does.
Only vertebrates have livers. (Does this mean you house the soul?)
    No wonder
Ancients centered emotions in you—so much larger than the heart, more
    sanguine and substantial
Than the brain. No wonder, to Crow Indians, mountain man Jeremiah
    "Liver-Eatin'" Johnson.
Was more powerful than if he'd been merely "Heart-Eatin'," "Brain-Eatin',"
    "Lung-Eatin'" Johnson.

Benedictions on the way blood percolates through you, Liver, en route
    from the intestines to the heart.
Benedictions on the way you catch and neutralize food additives, drugs,
    poisons, germs, excess sex hormones (too much of a good thing).
Benedictions on the way you store sugar as glycogen until it's needed,
    then reconvert it to sugar for energy.
Benedictions on the way you boost the blood with *albumin* (that keeps
    plasma from seeping

Through blood vessel walls), *fibrinogen* and *prothrombin* (that help
    blood clot),
Heparin (that keeps blood from clotting when it shouldn't), *globulin*
    (that fights infections).
Benedictions on the way you convert ammonia to *urea*, discharged
    in urine.
Benedictions on your production of bile, that green liquid that, despite
    medieval lies,
In fact improves the disposition, helping to break up globs of fat
    so that enzymes
In the intestine can convert them into fatty acids and glycerol which
    the body can use.
When red blood cells are destroyed in the bone marrow and spleen,
    and their hemoglobin
Dumped back into the blood, bless you, Liver, for accepting this crimson
    dye,
Transforming it to the folksily-named red *bilirubin* and green *biliverdin*
    that flow with the bile
Into the intestines, giving feces the brown color that warns our shoes
    away.

Astonishing, Liver, how you begin as a vestigal yolk sac.
    Astonishing
How a dense net of blood vessels, the *vitelline vessels*, develops in
    the yolk sac's wall.
How the *umbilical vessels* develop to bring nourishment from
    the uterus.
How both sets of vessels join behind the heart, and enter in like lovers
    holding hands.
How at this junction, capillaries create the *septum transversum*,
    with an outlet to the heart.
How cells detach from the "liver bay" in the gut, and the *mesothelium*,
    that lines the body cavity.
How these cells migrate to the *septum transversum*, surround
    the capillaries, and become liver cells.
How a human liver has four lobes: the large right one, the smaller left,
    and two much smaller lobes behind the right.

How each lobe is made of multi-sided lobules—50,000 to 100,000
    per adult liver.
How each lobule is one central vein surrounded by bundles or sheets
    of liver cells.
How cavities called *sinusoids* separate the cells, making the liver spongy,
    helping it hold blood.
How *sinusoids* drain into the central veins, which join to form the *hepatic
    vein*, from which blood leaves the liver.
How the mature liver is a labyrinth of crooked hallways and long, thin,
    crooked rooms.

Forgive me, Liver, for the swill I've pumped through you. Please keep
    doing your fantastic work,
Dear red-brown friend. I'm so afraid of hepatitis, that inflames you and could
    kill me.
I'm so afraid of cirrhosis, that turns you into yellow scar tissue, making you
    contract and fail.
I'm so afraid of cancer that chews you from the inside out, and jaundice,
    when the blood contains
Too much *bilirubin*, bringing about yellowing of the skin and eyes,
    warning
Of worse trouble to come. I'm so afraid of tuberculosis, dysentery, histo-
    plasmosis and syphilis
That start elsewhere but can take you over, Liver, the way kudzu has overrun
    the South.

You do much more for me every day than the Mayor. I think I should call you
    The Honorable Liver.
You do much more for me than the Governor. Liver for Governor. Liver
    for President. Liver for King.
I'd say "Liver for God," except you may already be. Hail Liver, full of grace.
    Our Liver who art in Heaven.
Organ of life, playing better than Bach the toccatas and fugues of good
    health and vitality,
Organ whose name contains the injunction to live, O Liver, O great One-
    Who-Lives, so we can too.

Neuroanatomy

The fog over the boulevard
    a thick cerebral cortex;
I enter its folds, its sulci and gyri;
      the canyons beneath me,
like ventricles; dusk
    seeps from them like dark fluids.

        *   *   *

On a stretched canvas,
8 brains neatly arranged.
Over each, a cartoon cloud
emptied of image or speech.
Whose brain was this
that I weigh in my hands,
heavy, dense as bread dough,
but porous?
We lift orange stick
and scalpel, begin
our dissection.

        *   *   *

Memory is probably stored chemically,
      in the synapse,
microscopic gap that is Lethe's antithesis;
    molecules ferry across
      rivers of remembering,
reversing Charon's way,
        between axon and dendrite.

        *   *   *

What we loved,
   where we have lived, lost
   in the layers of white.

        *   *   *

Where the boulevard reaches
            the north gate,
        the fog is so thick:
                    memories encountered in my office,
        the lives under shifting layers
of opacity. Images,
            as when the sun rises
and a gray house, a white fence,
        the branches of an oak appear;
                    or on a foggy street, suddenly,
a woman in a raincoat . . .

                    *   *   *

Folded within the neocortex
            are the gray masses
        regulating impulse and feeling;
as under the recent hills,
            tectonic plates and magma;
        the dissection proceeds but not
                    to the layers we dream from.

                    *   *   *

While it was whole,
            before we had peeled off
        the blood vessels and meninges,
                    and prepared to invade the cortex,
I held it up; whose brain?
            peeled off the cranial nerves:
olfactory, optic, oculomotor . . . ,
        to the tenth, the vagus,
                    meaning *wanderer.*

                    *   *   *

There's a party in the lab;
parts of the brain
are scattered on my lap, my jeans,

among chocolate cake crumbs and icing;
smelling of formaldehyde,
we sing Happy Birthday,
eat cake, resume our dissection.

*   *   *

I plummet through the folds
      of the cortex;
    thought, poem, terrors
        and longings murmured in my office:
electrical charges across the thin membranes
        between inside and out.

*   *   *

The professor, a woman, says,
    "The *massa intermedia,*
    one of the nerve bundles that joins
    the left and right hemispheres,
    is absent at autopsy from 85%
    of the male cadavers,
    and 15% of the female cadavers;
    nothing whatsoever is known
    of its function; no funding
    to solve the mystery of what it does."

Over our dissecting trays,
    the women laugh, the men
      look bewildered.

*   *   *

Where fog is as thick as fatty sheaths
of myelin over axons,
I go deeper in. How different from maps,
from procedures by daylight;
the studied structures, unrecognizable;
of what use, atlases of anatomy
when what in the text seemed merely complex,

turns out to have neighboring and overlapping structures,
idiosyncratic convolutions,
no color codes or little plastic flags with names?

*   *   *

In the lab, the familiar mass,
    lifted from its plastic bucket
and wet cheesecloth, menaces;
       later, the familiar road
          turns odd under the winter shadows
of what I'd imagined once
    to be merely eucalyptus and pine.

DENISE DUHAMEL

Facing My Amygdala

I take out my brain and put it in my lap.

I'm in search of my amygdala.

First I have to pass my cerebral cortex,
an ancient silvery eel that folds back onto itself.
My hypothalamus floats by like red peppercorn, giving
my brain spicy ideas—my cerebellum suddenly sexy
like a flower opening its pink legs. My pituitary gland
is only the size of a garbanzo bean, but it has
a lot of influence,
you can tell. It lives next to what I've been looking for,
what scientists claim is my center of fear.

My amygdala is oval, tiny and pale. Hard to imagine
it has given me so much trouble all these years.
I put on my glasses to get a better look. Inside
I see the subway
at midnight, large pointed teeth, all my failures,
the one I love leaving me for a blond with long legs.

My fears are so crowded they pile on top of each other.
The ones at the apex are trying to climb over the wall
of my almond-sized amygdala. The Empty Bank Account
steps on the back of Everybody's Laughing At Me
and grunts *one two three* and is gone. My Senile Parents
In A Poorly Run Nursing Home are catapulted by There's
Nothing
After Death. At the conclusion of three graceful
midair somersaults,
Mom and Dad land on their feet and make a run for it,
pulling translucent tubes out from their noses,
their gray hair quickly turning back to brown.
They slide down my spinal cord like firefighters
rushing to a blaze.

I try to touch my amygdala with the tip of my teaspoon,
but the utensil's too big and I am too clumsy.

So I pick up a lobster fork, hoping I can pluck out the fears
that now huddle together like patrons at a bank
during a robbery in progress. *Hey, you* need *some of us,*
a tentative voices says. *I mean, you* have *to be afraid
of things like knives in electrical outlets and men
coming at you with guns.*
Who do you think's responsible for fight or flight? I shout
to Fear of Getting Fat, *Hey, what about you? Certainly
you don't need
to hang around these creeps.* But she clings to her sister
Fear of Aging And Sagging Breasts, both chattering
their miniscule teeth.

Come on, Fear of Cancer. Loosen up! I go for my yearly exam.
No one in our immediate family has it.
He calls back in a voice so low and depressed I can
barely make it out:
*What about your mother's sister? What about
your father's brother?*
*What about their colons and lungs? What about
the fact that you grew up in a factory town*
where incidents of cancer are among the highest in the U.S.?
I remind Fear of Cancer I eat oat bran and vegetables,
drink bottled water,
never smoke a cigarette . . . Cutting me off, he says, *Sure,
right,*
Nuclear Disaster, Toxic Waste and Salmonella,
whispering and tsk-ing, *Don't listen to her. What
does she know?*

I go to talk to the medulla oblongata, the pointed
fleshy tongue
that's in charge of my breathing and heartbeat and digestion.
She says that my fears are making things hard for her,
that I gasp for air in the middle of the night,

that I have too many
bad dreams, that even the basal ganglia has complained
that I should be out in the world, getting more exercise,
but Fear of Crime doesn't want me running in the park alone.
When I confront my fears they grow more afraid. I can tell
they talk about me as soon as I leave the room.

I put my brain back on when Fear of Catching A Cold
starts fake-sneezing, the rest of my fears accusing me
of being a big bully,
Fear of Not Being Liked screeching as though she's being
stuck with pins.

I look up at the stars later on that clear black
and white night—
the Ursa Major, Canis Minor, the baseball diamond
of Delphinus.
I tell all my pretty fears, *Look! A God who made all this
surely must love each of us*, but even as I sing to myself
I feel my blood and bones off-key. My Fear
of Getting Pregnant
taunts me. I'm circled by Fear of AIDS
and Fear of Rape, both drunk again with messy beards.
And I wonder how long it will take

for all my fears to escape and where they'll go,
if they'll take up residence in my knees or my back
or my feet,
if they'll dissipate in the dirt after I'm buried.
Or if they'll be forever lost like my loose forgotten eyelash
blown from my cheek by my lover's breath,
the lover I'm most afraid to lose.

THOMAS LUX

The Limbic System

> *(from* limbus: *an edge, fringe, or border)*

The brain matter beneath the brain stem
and millimeters below the neocortex: imprecisely
defined, mysterious, no one
expert enough to know
for sure but having to do
with the visceral,
the emotional status of the organism: fear
and anger,
flight and defense, sense
of smell. . . . One part called *gyrus fornicatus*
and others called hippocampus,
uncus, amygdala. It is an injustice
that only neuro-doctors
get to say these words
and visit these places, map them, decode them.
And yet we all live there
where it is most primal, neurons firing
like starbursts, like the first flint
struck at night by hand on another stone—we all
live there near an edge,
just across the border
from another country,
the next: time.

ROALD HOFFMANN

What We Have Learned about the Pineal

Descartes knew, being, knew
that so central an organ confined
mechanism and mind, entwined.
But the gland held back being

of use, except to lizards, who,
(Descartes liked dissection)
deprived of it couldn't change
skin's tint. In man it calcifies

to an X-ray beacon, and that is
all we could do with this small
centrality, till Aaron Lerner,
awash in kilos of bovine pineals,

extracted melatonin, N-acetyl-
5-methoxytryptamine, a mine
of a name, a hormone that did
bleach tadpoles. In lampreys,

the tuatara, the gland rises
on a thin stalk from the brain,
an unblinking eye just below
the skin. But our pineal, light

insensitive, just pours out
melatonin all the time, more
in the dark so in diurnal rhyme,
seasons timed in chemical levels.

Some depressions are eased
by bright light. In hamsters
melatonin sets sex cycles, but
J. Arendt says: "... given to normal

subjects at a time of day (late
afternoon) calculated to maximize

any sexually related effects,"
just makes them sleepy. So not

the seat of the soul, but still
a gland to reckon with, a gland
to tell time. Descartes died
of a fever in Queen Christina's
sunshorn February Sweden.

Some of the material in this poem derived from an article
by Josephine Arendt in *New Scientist,* 25 July 1985, p. 36.

PATTIANN ROGERS

The Brain Creates Itself

A thread of tissues takes shape
As I first comprehend the red rock crossed twice
By the fringe-toed lizard at dusk.
A unique chain of cells becomes actual
As I identify the man beneath the white beech
And his influence on the nesting kiwi bird.

A new vein of reactions must arise
With my discovery of the dark star
On the rim of Sirius. A split-second network
Must be brought into being as I find the African
Dung beetle's egg buried in the elephant bolus.
And for each unacknowledged aspect of the purple
Spikenard beside the marsh-elder-to-be, for each unrecognized
Function of the ogre-faced stick spider at dawn,
A potential neuron is absent in the frontal lobe.

Imagine the molecular structure I create
As I contemplate the Galapagos dragon
At the bottom of the ocean stopping his heart
At will, dying for three minutes motionless
In the suck and draw of the sea. Imagine,
When I study his rapid zigzag swagger to the surface,
How a permanent line like silver makes its way
From the inner base of my skull to the top of my head.

And as I look at your face, following the contours
From your forehead to your chin, coming back again
To your eyes, I can almost picture the wide cranial
Web developing as my definite affection
For these particulars.

Cybernetics

Now you are ready to build your human brain.
You have studied the plan, and taken inventory
Of all the pieces you found in the kit.
The first brain won't be inexpensive or
Compact; covering most of Central Park
With these tiny transistors, it will cost
A sum slightly in excess of the Gross
National Product for Nineteen Fifty-Nine;
But that is not a scientific problem,
For later brains will reproduce themselves
At less expense, on a far smaller scale,
Bringing down average costs in the long run.
Screwdriver ready? But before you start,
Consider, helmsman, what a brain requires.
A human brain has always needed blood,
And always got it, too, in plenty; but
That problem occupies a later stage;
Right now, some elementary decisions.

It must, of course, be absolutely free,
That's been determined, and accordingly
You will program it to program itself,
Set up its own projects and work them out,
Adjusting what it does tomorrow by
The feedback from today, and casually
Repairing yesterday's disasters with
The earliest possible editorials.
It must assure itself, by masterful
Administration of the unforeseen,
That everything works according to plan,
And that, as a General from the Pentagon
Recently told Congress, "The period
Of greatest danger lies ahead." This way
Alone it will be able to preserve

Anxiety and sloth in a see-saw balance,
Provoking the flow of both adrenalin
And phlegm (speaking electronically),
Whence its conflicting elements achieve
A fair symbiosis, something between
The flood of power and the drouth of fear:
A mediocrity, or golden mean,
Maybe at best the stoic *apatheia*.

At the same time, to be a human brain,
It has to have a limiting tradition,
Which may be simple and parochial
(A memory of Main Street in the sunlight)
But should be unequivocal as well:
"My country right or wrong," or "I believe
In free enterprise and high tariffs,"
Or "God will punish me if I suck my thumb."
Something like that. You will provide also
A rudimentary view of history:
One eyeless bust of Cicero or Caesar,
A Washington Crossing the Delaware,
The Driving of the Golden Railroad Spike;
Maybe a shot of Lenin tombed in glass.
It need not be much, but it must be there.

Maybe you want a more ambitious brain?
One that can keep all history in mind,
Revise the whole to fit one added fact,
And do this in three hundredths of a second
While making accurate predictions of
Price fluctuations for the next six months?
Perfectly possible, and well within
The technical means at hand. Only, there's this:
It runs you into much more money for
Circuits of paradox and contradiction.
Your vessels of antinomian wrath alone

Run into millions; and you can't stop there,
You've got to add at every junction point
Auxiliary systems that will handle doubt,
Switches of agony that are On and Off
At the same time, and limited-access
Blind alleys full of inefficient gods
And marvelous devils. No, you're asking the
Impossible, Dostoevsky described it:
"A Petersburg intellectual with a toothache."
Better to settle for the simpler model.
You could put a man on the moon for less.

O helmsman! in your hands how equal now
Weigh opportunity and obligation.
A chance to mate those monsters of the Book,
The lion and serpent hidden from our sight
Through centuries of shadowed speculation.
What if the Will's a baffled, mangy lion,
Or Thought's no adder but a strong constrictor?
It is their offspring that we care about,
That marvelous mirror where our modest wit
Shall show gigantic. Will he uproot cities,
Or sit indoors on a rainy day and mope?
Will he decide against us, or want love?
How shall we see him, or endure his stride
Into our future bellowing Nil Mirari
While all his circuits click, propounding new
Solutions to the riddle of the Sphinx?

ALBERT GOLDBARTH

Vestigial

1. Appendix, Coccyx, Pineal Eye

Yes: that fingery fraction of a rabbit's commodious
sack, for the slow incorporating of cellulose: is
with us. The slinky bone-links of a tail have fused like flutes
into a panpipes: and are with us. And the lizard's
third, glazed eye is, like a whole yolk, folded
deep in the dough of our brains: and is awake there when
its outer brothers drowse. And there are some of us with
the tent flap vestige of vaginal lips around the standard
penis; with three-teated breasts . . . Or the One and a
Halfs: with parasite baby- "brother" or -"sister" bodies
dangling partway out: Laloo the Hindu: arms,
waist, buttocks, legs, "and perfect nails on the feet" extending forever
from his chest like a child burrowing in him, the head already
whispering to his lungs; it could pee and get hard. And
saying "freak" of them can't naysay what the gill and apehair
stages of the womb mean: everybody's wagged the tag-end of a fish
in the motherly waters. Do we know it, do we dream
the dreams of penguin, ostrich, rhea, kiwi, cassowary,
moa, rail, kakapo: all, birds for which flying's
a pair of muscley nubbins itching the living flesh.

2. The Adventures of John Dee

Not that an omelet of ostrich eggs intensifies
our own ties to the psyche of that African bird. Or
would he have thought exactly that?—John Dee,
astrologer and mage to the court of Elizabeth, himself
the wide-eyed vestige of an older world where poesie
and scientific method were a single creature romping
under planets, seraphs, meteor showers, ghosts. He
conjured ghosts. The Prince of Portugal ate ostrich eggs and
gave the shells to study: they were painted with the travel

of the heavenly spheres as agreeably authored by God and
telescope observation. Newton was around the corner.
Dee created a series of ten enormous "moonlight
towers," flashing war news for the Emperor Rudolph all
the way to Prague. And when the last faint light was
understood, and then slipped off its mirror, what did Dee think
in a darkened room of scrolls and crystals? Aubrey was around
the corner, scrutinizing megaliths. This final moment
Stonehenge still might be the footstools giants left. Dee
lifted a dinosaur bone. It might be Noah's, he thought, this
trace of a time when stature matched faith and accomplishment.

3.   Big Bang

Ooohing over Stonehenge—over skew-silhouetted
Egyptian gods, or Hopi sand mandalas—finally
recognizes not what's different but what's essentially
us in them. And so we flock to Laloo and his atavistic cohorts,
Alligator Lady, Monkey Boy, to see their fairground skins containing
ordinary life. They wink and sip their scotch. They marry. When
The Human Frog and Mule Woman wed, Sabine the Serpent Girl was
maid of honor—then godmother seven times. They only made the same
attempt as anyone you know, to be the wheel Plato says
we all were in the days when man and woman formed a single-bodied
being rolling breezily over the world. I think that's why
at night, some nights, we see the stars in their terrible solitude
and systems of attachment: as a sign for what our lives are:
smithereens on fire, having been exploded from our wholeness
and our source. That may be accurate cosmology or not. I
only know I've walked the darkness wanting more than any
Stonehenge to align with something bright. And then the lunar
dole of remnant sunlight touched me—here: an x between
the shoulderblades, those made-for-raising things. They stirred. Not
wings, no. More like the fossils of wings.

ALBERT GOLDBARTH

The Sciences Sing a Lullabye

Physics says: go to sleep. Of course
you're tired. Every atom in you
has been dancing the shimmy in silver shoes
nonstop from mitosis to now.
Quit tapping your feet. They'll dance
inside themselves without you. Go to sleep.

Geology says: it will be alright. Slow inch
by inch America is giving itself
to the ocean. Go to sleep. Let darkness
lap at your sides. Give darkness an inch.
You aren't alone. All the continents used to be
one body. You aren't alone. Go to sleep.

Astronomy says: the sun will rise tomorrow,
Zoology says: on rainbow-fish and lithe gazelle,
Psychology says: but first it has to be night, so
Biology says: the body-clocks are stopped all over town
and
History says: here are the blankets, layer on layer, down and down.

ROALD HOFFMANN

Jerry-Built Forever

1

We think that all that matters
can't be deep, but chunk-to-
knowledge-chunk in subsurface
veins, and we, mind-armed miners

search/dance to lift earth cover,
free the plan. The world, oh it
waits patiently to be known,
and we do know much: what

the bombardier beetle sprays;
the salts, silts and organics,
the gradients in the Azov
sea; far bangs and dodges

of light in space; how vitamin
B_{12} twists one pyrrole ring
as it is made. Terra incog-
nita shrunk to the way the birch

bark peels and why he dressed
in white the night he sealed
the garage door cracks and
turned on the engine . . .

2

This biconcave bialy platelet
of the erythrocyte, the red
heart of the blood, holds the oxygen
carrier, hemoglobin. Four coiled

polypeptide chains, four subunits
changing pairwise twice in the fetus
to let it soak up placental O_2
steadily. Each chain a globular

protein, juxtaposed twining
of helical segments, predestined
kinks, sequences of amino acids
alike in sperm whale and horse,

a meander of bonds around
the flat disc that colors all . . . heme,
the active site, the oxygen binding
site, a porphyrin, iron. Oxygen,

enflamer, winds to a pocket
molded by protein, binds iron, moves
it in consummation, chains
tethering heme tense—a far

subunit feels the first heme's bond
quiver, the chains pull, O_2 binds
easier. Cooperativity, an allosteric
protein. In 1937

not long before the war,
Felix Haurowitz watched crystals
of deoxyhemoglobin
shatter on oxygenation.

3

Beauty whirls rococo
in fussy chains round
the oxygen pocket; beauty
cambers simple—the iron

hub of heme. If God's
plan for all this function
be heresy, at least let
what came, chanced, to be

be best. Heme, myo- and hemo-
globins, vertebrates' O_2

transport proteins, subunits'
trim fit link—evolved.

4

Carried by blood, carrying
electrons, life-empowering
oxygen. Elsewhere, in engines
it's sucked into carburetor

trains, there to mix with branched
heptanes, octanes, another kind
of feedstock. Sparked, it burns
things in controlled explosions,

a human specialty. And what
thermochemistry says should end
in greening CO_2 and steam, in
incomplete combustion partly

goes to CO, carbon monoxide.
This odorless diatomic tres-
passer sweeps into bronchia, brashly
binding 200 times better

than O_2. A free ride on deoxyhemo-
globin down arteries, right past
cells that long for the other, can't
wait too long before shutdown.

5

So a life ends. That wise blood,
a million years in the making, it
should have fought, that oxygen-
starved blood. But Nature's

a tinkerer, a shanty-town contractor,
filer of misfit gears, the original

found artist. In oxygenated
salty soups, lightning-lit, when

molecules swam to be shaped,
and vines groped for the sun, she
took anything that worked, or the first
that passed the million destructions

of her sweet time lab. No white-
coated intelligences to hurry her
or remind her of the carbon
monoxide that was not there.

This poem owes much to an article by F. Jacob in *Science*
(vol. 196, 1161, 1977). Actually there "always" has been some
CO there, produced in the body in the course of normal
breakdown processes. Hemoglobin and myoglobin bind CO
some 100 times less strongly than their component, heme.
Presumably the oxygen-carrying mechanism evolved so as
to be able to function adequately with the little amount of
physiological CO around, and to do that it actually had to *suppress* the CO-binding capability of the heme group. A shaped
protein pocket does that. For more on these wondrous proteins
see L. Stryer, *Biochemistry*, 3d ed. (New York: W. H. Freeman
and Co., 1988), chapter 7.

D. A. FEINFELD

Skeleton Key

FOR DR. THOMAS SCULCO

Skin is an illusion,
flesh wearies and fails;
the lens of decades looks only
at a naked skeleton.

The print of sex unites,
divides us in the womb:
hips take a certain twist,
pinching or spreading caliper thighs
that span begetting and birthing.

Bone outlasts
our temporary muscles
after a life is picked clean,
white surface scrimshawed
by time's needle
that stitches together our days.

Icicles melt, drip deep
in the sinews—layers
over last night's ruins remember
the breaking and making whole;
grinding of years
scores joint sockets,
like convict-scratches on cell walls.

Seven Stages of Skeletal Decay

0-5   Centers of ossification appear as I squall
"wyde in this world wonderes to hear."
The light my second amnion.
Mother like a frog, white exhausted thighs
precede my deciduous teeth, the better to bite
the asylum where I didn't earn my keep.
Ward of the state and stable criteria.

5-12   Acetabular elements join.
Ilium, ischium, pubis,
a little hen's breast against my hands.
In the corpulent dark, hearing children grow
a song of bones as the moon climbed
and ovary bells, my eggs and the moon
tolling each month.

12-25   Epiphysial union of long bones.
Long bones in my stride,
glib nights, counterfeit smiles,
trumped-up charges against what I loved.
Years blindly eating childhood's fat.
Knowledge like a shield
wounds when pressed too near.

25-36   Active vault suture closing.
Active designs in the skull.
Delicate zippers sealing in
the stars, interstellar dust,
brackets of marriage, and one short birth
shaped like a comma between two worlds.

36-50   Lipping of scapular glenoid fossa.
Fossa, a ditch.
I have not come to it.
Fossa, an abyss.
I wait for the master archeologist

to dig and pick,
tweezers plucking artifacts,
my trail of refuse and souvenirs.

50 plus Quasi pathological erosions of bone.
The pendulum's pit.
My old electrons blow their fuse.
Dark pond.
My mother like a frog,
white exhausted thighs collapsed.

plus What did it mean to play
a xylophone of bones?
An octave of stone. Delight. Decrease,
bleached lips dim against my fingers
closing in a stiffening fist,
dumb warrior
pitted against eloquent death,
illiterate mulch for those whose squalls
will go "wyde in this world
wonderes to hear,"
the light their second amnion.

9

Theory and Speculation

. . . where dream is logic

ALBERT GOLDBARTH

STEPHANIE STRICKLAND

Presto! How the Universe Is Made

On your Mark, one first O/riginal Form; *Get set,* a second
angular Segment; *Go*—the next step, a Rule replacing
each straight side in the first by the second; if I take

a box and for each side of that box substitute a cone
or peak, to make a kind of star—then do *again*
what I did before: take the star-box

and where I find a straight-line replace it
with a peak, to make a *starrier* star, nesting the shape
even deeper in the figure, re-placing

peaks to make a Star-in-the-Box! Or, a Diamond-heart-
Star at *every* level (a shape self-similar); a shape
of extreme complication, in only a few—in five—

iterations, it already reads as texture and is rapidly
sinking as it plummets, repeating, into bonded
lock, where photons mediate, shunting between

heavy center, vibrant orbit. Or *deeper,* look. No,
look, a quantum leap: the burst box—the born star—is re-
emerging on the line, on the line *or/and.* . . . . Repeat:

The Leaves of a Dream Are the Leaves of an Onion

1

Red oak leaves rustle in the wind.
Inside a dream, you dream the leaves
scattered on dirt, and feel it
as an instance of the chance configuration

to your life. All night you feel
red horses galloping in your blood,
hear a piercing siren, and are in love
with the inexplicable. You walk

to your car, find the hazard lights
blinking: find a rust-brown knife, a trout,
a smashed violin in your hands.
And then you wake, inside the dream,

to find tangerines ripening in the silence.
You peel the leaves of the dream
as you would peel the leaves off an onion.
The layers of the dream have no core,

no essence. You find a tattoo of
a red scorpion on your body.
You simply laugh, shiver in the frost,
and step back into the world.

2

A Galapagos turtle has nothing to do
with the world of the neutrino.
The ecology of the Galapagos Islands
has nothing to do with a pair of scissors.
The cactus by the window has nothing to do
with the invention of the wheel.
The invention of the telescope

has nothing to do with a red jaguar.
No. The invention of the scissors
has everything to do with the invention of the telescope.
A map of the world has everything to do
with the cactus by the window.
The world of the quark has everything to do
with a jaguar circling in the night.
The man who sacrifices himself and throws a Molotov
cocktail at a tank has everything to do
with a sunflower that bends to the light.

3

Open a window and touch the sun,
or feel the wet maple leaves flicker in the rain.
Watch a blue crab scuttle in clear water,
or find a starfish in the dirt.
Describe the color green to the color blind,
or build a house out of pain.

The world is more than you surmise.
Take the pines, green-black, slashed by light,
etched by wind, on the island
across the riptide body of water.
Describe the thousand iridescent needles
to a blind albino Tarahumara.

In a bubble chamber, in a magnetic field,
an electron spirals and spirals in to the center,
but the world is more than such a dance;
a spiraling in to the point of origin,
a spiraling out in the form of a
wet leaf, a blue crab, or a green house.

4

The heat ripples ripple the cactus.
Crushed green glass in a parking lot

or a pile of rhinoceros bones
give off heat, though you might not notice it.

The heat of a star can be measured
under a spectrometer, but not
the heat of the mind, or the heat of Angkor Wat.
And the rubble of Angkor Wat

gives off heat; so do apricot blossoms
in the night, green fish, black bamboo,
or a fisherman fishing in the snow.
And an angstrom of shift turns the pleasure

into pain. The ice that rips the fingerprint
off your hand gives off heat;
and so does each moment of existence.
A red red leaf, disintegrating in the dirt,

burns with the heat of an acetylene flame.
And the heat rippling off
the tin roof of the adobe house
is simply the heat you see.

5

What is the secret to a Guarneri violin?
Wool dipped in an indigo bath turns bluer
when it oxidizes in the air. Marat is
changed in the minds of the living.
A shot of tequila is related to Antarctica
shrinking. A crow in a bar or red snapper on ice
is related to the twelve tone method
of composition. And what does the tuning of tympani
have to do with the smell of your hair?
To feel, at thirty, you have come this far—
to see a bell over a door as a bell
over a door, to feel the care and precision
of this violin is no mistake, nor is the
sincerity and shudder of passion by which you live.

6

Crush an apple, crush a possibility.
No single method can describe the world;
therein is the pleasure
of chaos, of leaps in the mind.
A man slumped over a desk in an attorney's office
is a parrot fish caught in a seaweed mass.
A man who turns to the conversation in a bar
is a bluefish hooked on a cigarette.
Is the desire and collapse of desire in an unemployed carpenter
the instinct of salmon to leap upstream?
The smell of eucalyptus can be incorporated
into a theory of aggression.
The pattern of interference in a hologram
replicates the apple, knife, horsetails on the table,
but misses the sense of chaos, distorts
in its singular view. Then
touch, shine, dance, sing, be, becoming, be.

Reality Organization

1.

4:30 A.M. with the woe adding up
in notches on your gut-wall,
guilts, indignities, whatever, there's no sleep,
you're bright, you "keep up," you know what's what, but
this isn't the time when you want to know everything's nothing

but some few subatomic elements skeetering
through emptiness, what seem the solid edges of things
are hazinesses of particle give-and-take and "really"
must look like continual maelstrom, and people you love
are whole new sets of cells each 7 years—no,

that's all fine to know but now you simply want
to walk with some dignity to the shed, and
press your forehead to the russian olive there, its trunk
unyielding, a thing not you but able to texture you,
a hardness to hold to, a firm true specific event.

2.

Zen and the Art of Computer Management Systems.
Holistic Bioengineering: A Home Cassette Series.
Alternate Consciousness and Corporation Profile—A Symposium.
By now it's no secret: scientific method,
the Newtonian/Cartesian paradigm, isn't hauling ass

and soul in happy tandem very well. And so
(as one book says) "to use an obvious example," war
we calibrate down to the leastmost ladybug's-waist-sized
chainmail link and up to megaton trajectory, we
artfully assemble, Trojan H and H-bomb, but

what makes us make war, what demanding psyche-ghosts
howl down the spiral staircase

of our genes—"we are no closer to this
understanding now than, say, in Hellenistic times." They
had *Lysistrata*. We have biofeedback and we have *Lysistrata*.

3.

We have biofeedback. We know there are levels
where light's too large to land, so "being" anything isn't
being visible or countable—levels where dream is
logic, levels where you could fall lost in the space
between your own hand and its shadow. Maybe a God,

even a God of terrible vengeance, is less frightening
than floating through physics. The God says:
Here are boundaries; this and this are real, this not.
The God says: Things actually do add up. We love
to add. The name of Allah was *26,000*

times stitched into a 16th century Turkish warship's pennant.
There are an estimated *4 million* mummified ibises
in an Egyptian labyrinth offered unto Thoth.
We love to tally. The rosary's abacus beads.
The first worked stones are scored.

4.

It was nearly dawn when I found you. By then
you were calm. That tree had punished you or healed you
or simply been a symbol of something reliably
beyond the tormenting refinements of human confusion.
Your skin was moire from the bark—your sadness,

leached out by that contact. I led you back
into the house. Or you could have been leading me—that's
not the point. I know we can't approach the universe
as if its secrets are quantifiable, not any more. And even
so, I know we all deserve the reassurance

of weight and number, perimeter, durability. Some
days both of those opposing knowings pull, and early
sun in a slant through the basketball net
mandalas the shed—my eyes can spin in there,
electronwise, wholegalaxyclusterwise, and not be wiser.

Architecture

A restless trafficking in parts is the hallmark
of building an embryo, whatever the species.
  Natalie Angier*

So then is Nature just a toddler sorting Legos,
puzzling out how the pieces fit, until something
a young-ancient mind can recognize suggests
itself—a house, a horse. Change one element,
you get a whole different object. But once fixed,
prophecy becomes paradigm, the fall-back pattern
we enact while congratulating ourselves on
the refinement of our latticework.

It is no news
that we have to reinvent ourselves
again and again.
Unless we've already given up,
the light over the drawing board
is always on. We suppose.

Biology confirms myth.
(Can't you see it as a headline?)
Oracular Apollo ordered "Know thyself"
inscribed on the wall of his Delphic temple.
Finally, we discover what he meant.

While we sit on our balconies,
sipping red wine,
plotting the next millennium,
on the subcellular level
our genomes are milling about,
confused, trying to find out
who they are.

*from "Heads or Tails? How Embryos Get It Right,"
New York Times, 21 November 1995, pp. C1 and 12.

MICHAEL L. JOHNSON

Schrödinger's Cat

FOR L.W.

The atomic decay has neither
happened nor not happened,
the cat has neither been
killed nor not killed, until
we look inside the box . . .
  John Gribbin, *In Search of Schrödinger's Cat*

Does the puzzle include its metaphor,
which seems to implicate Pandora's box
(the maternal womb, the unconscious itself)
or the casket whose contents must be guessed?

Is looking inside the box an attempt
to know darkness by turning on a light?

Or does the cat have too human a face?

If God plays dice, who dares write scripture? Can
the cards ever speak for themselves? And is
the game only what the referee sees?

How many universes *are* there, then?

Does the last question box another one
that, like Mme. de Vionnet, could take
all of our categories by surprise?

RENÉE OLANDER

Universe: Alter-Egos (A Meditation on Strange Attractors)

1. **Shapes and Sounds**

Here a windpipe down to a fiery core,
A churning liquid voice of burst star parts, iron ore
And lava hot can call a game—

Here a song of methane
Rises up from swamp scooped out and stuffed
With refuse cultures scattered over crust—

Somewhere cranky continents shift deep
Rear their bony limbs in buxom seas—

And seven seas, profane and holy,
Rise and fall like air in an ancient atmosphere—

Here a crawling voice of a globe drones clear
Under a din of light and smoke
Atoms and hearts, purring star parts—
Old matter, ancient species—
Particles infused with energy—
Water and sunlight, periodic chemistry.

Hear the groan of so many souls, centuries old,
Who bathe and bake under a ball
Of burning time, who bask
Anonymous as kin on Thanksgiving—

Listen: lean both ears:
Windy rhythms pour through leaves, green or crackling,
And ripple rivers and streams
Content as cats or humming
Traffic below city windows
Sucking and spewing exhaust.

Hear the near voices still plants seem to breathe—
Above the surface of this sphere, a sonorous blur
Spins and speeds.

2. **Dreams**

In a mind's eye, in a metal mirror, I see
How I carry my home in my head
And crawl along a crust
Of a small sphere in a minor galaxy—
And ever matter presses me
Warmly awake in the dark:

In rippling water, I see
A bent body, tall weeds,
Rainbow oils glistening—
Around me pavement leads
Bunches of bustling lives
Under hazy skies.

A seawall laps black-brown,
A sign reads 'No fishing'
And a rat as long as my right foot
Almost gets squashed in my stride.

(The rat's sunken black
Eyes buzz with flies
But its tail arcs in air
Like a paisley design.)

Once I stared at a glaring screen
And saw those sandpiles slipping
Off barges tugs push down polluted
Rivers were souls—ashen and common—

My sight dims, dependent on this tapered
Arm of a minor galaxy.

3. **You**

Close your face in hands and feel your bone
Beneath enfolding membrane—

Sometimes feel your hip sockets
Unlocking femurs in runs or jumps—
Feel your cord stiffen in tight spots
And jaws lock
Inside the muscles of your mask—

Feel your body beneath, inside, a frame and core, a plane—
How matter makes you
Atoms and energy
Burning and being in a mind's eye
While yawning jaw swings wide
And lips withdraw to teeth, gums, glistening tongue—
Magic muscle in this small country.

Feel your throat steer warm breath free
Without asking
And pull random samplings back
Into what seems a battery
Operated organism, half perhaps
A life yet charged—

Feel how womb tightens—
Feel heart and bowels—
Stomach churning meat or greens—

Feel the weight of the form you carry—
Milagro-machine more sure than you—
Your part and parcel—
Feel your iron rivers pulsing,
Your airways breathe like trees, unconsciously.

4.   **Strange Attractors**

Strange attractors puzzle me—
Weather patterns and EEGs
Conjure cool art on computer screens—
Peeling petals, rippling seeds
Original as chaos

Kicked up and settled as mythologies
Or the studies of sediment and stone.

Matter grows fat and hungry,
Licks and tastes new alchemies—
Glowing sludge and factories'
Excretions like huge species'
Corpses sunk in salty stews
Of everlasting opportunities
To be atoms, energy
Supple and crusty
As roots, reptiles, continents' caves—
Passageways
To the core of a small orb
Whose layers bake like pastries,
Even as heat
Sun sheds on dusty prairies—

My dry skin flakes like silicon
Sifted on the growing heap—
My tastebuds bloom as I eat
And waters and winds suck and seal me
In light years, in chaos, in chemistry—
Atoms, energy
Dapple spidery galaxies
And edges of minor minds.

BILL KNOTT

The Consolations of Sociobiology

Those scars rooted me. Stigmata stalagmite
I sat at a drive-in and watched the stars
Through a straw while the coke in my lap went
Waterier and waterier. For days on end or

Nights no end I crawled on all fours or in
My case no fours to worship you: Amoeba Behemoth!
—Then you explained your DNA calls for
Meaner genes than mine and since you are merely

So to speak its external expression etcet
Ergo among your lovers I'll never be . . .
Ah that movie was so faraway the stars melting

Made my thighs icy. I see: it's not you
Who is not requiting me, it's something in you
Over which you have no say says no to me.

Sea of Negative Charges

FOR HUGH POLAN

My father can make little sense of Chemistry. This is why I enjoy it, the barrier between foreign tongues. He doesn't know he should have been raised speaking Chemistry. His grammar school education should have ignored verbal constructions and gone straight to the formulas. Chemistry is everywhere. My father would have grown into a much happier man—perhaps not as old—if he had only learned to balance a chemical equation. He is puzzled when I mention that the reason he is such a good conductor of family matters, and yet so malleable, is his electron mobility. He allows most negative particles to slide past him. Chemistry might solve his bonding problems if he would examine his internal structure. Unknowingly, he exhibits what we call delocalized bonding; the attractions are there but with nowhere to go. If he spoke Chemistry, I could explain to him why he is always so tired, that bond formation is often an energy-releasing process—potential energy decreases as charges come closer together. I would tell him about forces and affinities, and then he might understand how chemists keep the world from falling apart, what seems to work in theory. It has nothing to do with mass or radioactive decay. It all comes down to reading the symbols and interpreting the data, keeping one eye on the instruments, holding back all possibilities for decomposition. Of course, Chemistry has never solved much of anything.

c = the physics of farewell

nothing we know can exceed the speed of light,
but death, i think, can carry its cargo off
almost as fast. remember einstein's rocket?
life and death are the famous twins, and no matter
how many times we perform this experiment,
i am the one who is always left behind,
growing older, waiting for your return.
far away you go and fast, and the farther
and faster you go, the younger you'll remain.
often at night when i see you, i can see how well
the experiment works: your skin so smooth, your hair
still fine and blond. yes, the experiment works; it
proves nothing more than itself, but damn, it works
and you are farther and faster away than ever
and einstein, once again, has been no help.
i understand everything now that's worth understanding
about time and distance. soon i'll be fifty. still
the experiment runs. i don't think i'll be here,
dear twin, for your return, but lucky's the world
that you'll be bringing your youth and beauty back to.

Thoughts near the Close of Millennium

In this expanding universe, everything is leaving everything,
    yet there is no center
From which any of this leave-taking leaves; the middle
    of every departure
Is everywhere. Microcosmically viewed, it all looks a lot like
    the pores of Dizzy Gillespie's cheeks
When he blew his horn. We're spinning away from the sun
    and the stars
While Ceres moves away from Jupiter and Neptune moves
    away from Mars.
Everything is leaving its immediate neighborhood, gathering
    more and more distance
For itself, like the furthest quasar, that—18 billion light years ago—
    said goodbye to Proxima Centauri.
Even Nancy down the street is leaving Charlie and the kids. Like
    everything else,
We're forever blown away by that first Big Bang. We're stuck
    in the atmospheric saddle
Of a slow-motion explosion, like that one at the end of Antonioni's
    Zabriskie Point,
Where that floating olive might be the earth, and if we slow down
    the slow-motion (slow it,
Geometrically, down), we can witness that olive decomposing
    and watch entropy eat it up
While we consider that all those little anatomizing volcanoes and
    olivequakes of it
Might be comparable to the shifting and colliding of continents
    which have slow-danced
To the music of the spheres for billions of summer nights, crashing
    their own weddings
And feasting off each others' tectonic plates until the next big bash:
    all of which is just the drop-of-an-olive
In a martini glass compared to what it would take to understand
    what I'm talking about

Is the energy that is the black hole of me that sucked this martini
    so dry that no light exists,
And now the pimento of that olive is the pit in my stomach
    which seems to have multiplied
In density a thousand-fold, like a pellet of buckshot become
    shot put,
Or maybe, like—at the core of a white dwarf—that teaspoon
    of matter that weighs five tons.
So maybe all this wonder and worry—and all this speculation—
    is futile, because, here it is,
New Year's Eve again and I don't think I need to overstate my
    point.

What If We Were Alone?

What if there weren't any stars?
What if only the sun and the earth
circled alone in the sky? What if
no one ever found anything outside
this world right here?—no Galileo
could say, "Look—it is out there,
a hint of whether we are everything."

Look out at the stars. Yes—cold
space. Yes, we are so distant that
the mind goes hollow to think it.
But something is out there. Whatever
our limits, we are led outward. We glimpse
company. Each glittering point of light
beckons: "There is something beyond."

The moon rolls through the trees, rises
from them, and waits. In the river all
night a voice floats from rock
to sandbar, to log. What kind of listening
can follow quietly enough? We bow, and
the voice that falls through the rapids
calls all the rocks by their secret names.

ROALD HOFFMANN

Grand Unification

This is just a rule; strings that meet,
wriggling in their roughened-up space-time,
if their tips just touch, they must merge,

and bigger lines, loops, necklaces or thatchings
self-assemble. This is so. But it is not real,
it's just a rule. Loops tangle, there is an exchange

of quantum numbers, the stray collision
sets the strings rotating, rippling, a whip
and then the extra snap looses a particle

(boson or fermion) and light, any color. The math
says it must be so. Mind you, this is not: people,
passing, a look that locks on some missed braid

of a future. This is not: a hummingbird's tie
to the sweet and red, tie testing stasis.
And it is not the interlace of frost, another

season's nonlinear history of steam meanders.
Nor: rope dancers . . . For those you need words.
But here just watch the math, follow it across

or around or down, just follow its unhusking
to the small world, where intuition is strung
out as far as it will give, but equations

work as well here as for real billiard balls,
whirling dervishes or galaxies (there is no need
for me to say all this). In this smallness infinities,

anomalies slough off, the loops vibrate, a keen
undulation, clockwise rippling nothingness
in ten dimensions. Twenty-six the other way.

This fits. But it's not all. The dimensions
must compactify, in a silent crumpling, curling
in of what there's room for, into inwards' innards.

The quantum numbers then come out naturally,
strung out on a loop that is gravity, the source
of all interactions. We are *so* near understanding

everything. I believe, reasons without words,
classy symmetries. It's a rule. And up scale the sun
shines, frost melts and zing! go the strings of my heart.

A. R. AMMONS

Prodigal

After the shifts and dis-
continuities, after the congregations of orders,
   black masses floating through
   mind's boreal clarity, icebergs in fog,
flotillas of wintering ducks weathering the night,
   chains of orders, multifilamentous chains
   knobbed with possibility, disoriented
chains, winding back on themselves, unwinding,
   intervolving, spinning, breaking off

(nomads clustering at dusk into tents of sleep,
disorganizing, widening out again with morning)
   after the mental

   blaze and gleam,
the mind in both motions building and tearing down,
   running to link effective chains,
   establish molecules of meaning,
frameworks, to
   perfect modes of structuring
   (so days can bend to trellising
and pruned take shape,
   bloom into necessary event)

   after these motions, these vectors,
orders moving in and out of orders, collisions
   of orders, dispersions, the grasp weakens,

   the mind whirls, short of the unifying
reach, short of the heat
   to carry that forging:

   after the visions of these losses, the spent
seer, delivered to wastage, risen
   into ribs, consigns knowledge to
   approximation, order to the vehicle
of change, and fumbles blind in blunt innocence
   toward divine, terrible love.

10

Number

Thus miracled infinity is viewed . . .

MICHAEL L. JOHNSON

LISEL MUELLER

Reasons for Numbers

1

Because I exist

2

Because there must be a reason
why I should cast a shadow

3

So that good can try to be better
and become best
and beginning grow into middle and end

4

So the round earth can have its corners
and the house will not fall down around me

So the seasons will go on holding hands
and the string quartet play forever

5

For the invention of Milton and Shakespeare
and the older invention
of the wild rose, mother
to the petals
of my hand

6

Because
five
senses
are

not
enough

7

Because luck
is always odd
and the division
of history
into lean and fat
                     years
mysterious

8

To make the spider
possible
and the black ball which tells me
the game is up

but also to let
the noise of the world
make itself heard
as music

9

For the orbit of Jupiter
                Saturn
                Venus
                Mars
                Mercury
                Uranus
                Mickey Mantle
                Lou Gehrig
                Babe Ruth

10

Created functionless, for the sheer play
of the mind in its tens of thousands of moves

There is nothing like it in nature

Integrals

> Erect, arched in disdain,
> the integrals drift from left
> across white windless pages
> to the right,
> serene as swans.
> Tall,
> beautiful seen from afar
> on the wavering water, each
> curves with the balanced severity
> of a fine tool weighed in the palm.
>
> Gaining energy now, they
> break into a canter—stallions
> bobbing the great crests of their manes.
> No one suspects their power
> who has not seen them rampage.
> Like bulldozers, they build
> by adding
> dirt to dirt to stumps added
> to boulders to broken glass added
> to live trees by the roots added
> to hillsides, to whole
> housing developments
> that roll, foaming before them,
> the tumbling end of a broken wave
> in one mangled sum: dandelions, old
> beer-cans and broken
> windows—gravestones all
> rolled into one.
>
> Yes, with the use of tables
> integration is as easy as that:
> the mere squeeze of a trigger, no
> second thought. The swans
> cannot feel the pain
> it happens so fast.

NADYA AISENBERG

Measures

The formless needs to be concealed.
Who dares summon demons
from their dissonant intervals,
risk shipwreck through miscalculation?
Number binds the order of the soul
and of the universe.
More than our days are numbered,
children of Kronos. Speech, step, song.
One rectangle so beautiful
men call it golden,
the Divine Proportion of the Parthenon.
The light years we wait to see the light.

CHARLES SIMIC

Ghost Stories Written

Ghost stories written as algebraic equations.
Little Emily at the blackboard is very frightened.
The X's look like a graveyard at night. The teacher
wants her to poke among them with a piece of
chalk. All the children hold their breath. The white
chalk squeaks once among the plus and minus
signs, and then it's quiet again.

SUE OWEN

Zero

This is the story of zero,
born to live a life
of emptiness, only
child of plus and minus.

Its bones invisible
so it could be seen through
like an eye.
With that vision, you could

see the past and future
and how they mimic each other.
At first, it was thought
the zero was a mouth

and would say something
profound to the numbers.
But added to them, it never
amounted to much, and

subtracted, it never wanted
to take anything away.
Zero was a sad case,
only wanted to master emotion

and silence like chess.
Each winter, the approaching
degrees never could locate
its cold, missing heart.

Boolean Algebra: $X^2 = X$

Quantity is what is not. The truth
is ignorant of numbers. The universe
is one, is all; besides there is nothing. The square
of one, the square of nothing, is only one,
—or nothing. X^2 equals X. The truth
admits these values. What is other is not
the truth. Zero and one. An algebra
of these alone expresses everything.

But Boole was wrong; his formulas were wrong,
as Euclid was, as Newton, anyone.
Ingenious Boole. Wasn't his passion right,
that offered him to universal form
though it eluded him? One has such joy
to look at the mind of man, frail, deep
in disorder, always pushed by the falsenesses
of unreality, confined in the dark
of all we never know, yet strong with a greed
for form, the fact of which we lust toward,
believing, however often the substance is lost—
one has such joy here, it is as though
an amoeba should read to us, or snakes should sing.

COLE SWENSEN

New Math

As if the word everything
meant everything
as all words do.
We refer again to prosopognosia*—
that condition in which
the victim cannot distinguish
between faces.
If we could compute the numerical value
of a turning wrist, a sense of shock,
toast on a plate,
paint by number
one picture in a single dimension.
Both portrait and landscape
can trace their ancestry
back to the point.
If every breath
is a separate equation
and yet they all equal zero,
that egg with a vacuum inside,
the insensible which we
sense and call invisible
has succeeded in imaging a new circle,
imagine
any thing in which
each point lies the same
distance from every other.

*The word *prosopognosia* is taken from *Left Brain, Right Brain* by
Sally P. Springer and Georg Deutsch (W. H. Freeman, 1981). It is
the name of a specific type of aphasia—the inability to recog-
nize faces.

Fractals*

> *Euclid alone has looked on beauty bare*
> Edna St. Vincent Millay

Euclid alone began to formulate
the relation of circle, plane and sphere
in equations making it quite clear
it was symmetry that we must contemplate.

He left the jagged convoluted form,
rambling rivers, wind turbulence and rain;
ignored clouds, coastline and storms,
and the whorl of tree, skin and terrain,

to map the triangle, cone and square.
Euclid measured order and left the knot
of chaos to be unraveled by Mandelbrot
who found truth in the course of blood and air.
Euclid looked on beauty stark and bare,
but Mandelbrot appraised her everywhere.

*a geometry invented in 1975 by Benoit Mandelbrot to find order in
chaotic shapes and processes

PATTIANN ROGERS

Fractal: Repetition of Form over a Variety of Scales

This moment is a single blue jay,
a scramble of flint, sapphire iron,
spiking blue among the empty brambles
and vines wound like skeins back
upon themselves through the dun forest
of thistle spurs and thorns.

And this moment is as well the brambled
skeleton of the jay, anthracite spine,
thorny blades and femurs, tangle
of knuckled twigs flittering
through an equal flitter of jointed
sticks, fines and husks of wind.

And as well again, this split second
is the single blue-black pod of jay heart
thiddering among a bramble of rib bones
inside the tufts, the bristled
capsules of forest and winter barbed
and strung with dusk.

And the jay's call is this same
instant, a cry of release slivered
and shaped by the tangle of bones
and scrub woods, by the bolus wound
of winter air, thatched and spurred,
through which it travels.

And this moment is a single point
of sun wrapped and templing in the black
pathways of the blue jay's eye, like a heart
shuddering in a tangle of bones,
like a bird in a shifting knot of forest,
a call in a skeletal patch of winter,
winter in a weaving clutch of dusk, a moment

tangling within the string and bristle
of its own vocabulary.

God is a process, a raveled nexus
forever tangling into and around the changing
form of his own moment—pulse and skein,
shifting mien, repeating cry
of loss and delivery.

ROBERT FRAZIER

A Fractal Pattern

> *The importance of fractals lies in their ability to capture the*
> *essential features of very complicated and irregular objects and*
> *processes, in a way that is susceptible to mathematical analysis.*
>   Benoit Mandelbrot

> *They said, "You have a blue guitar,*
> *You do not play things as they are."*
> *The man replied, "Things as they are*
> *Are changed upon the blue guitar."*
>   Wallace Stevens

The crystalline structures step,
    soldiers in perfect rule,
down to the vanishing point
    of any metallic molecule:
self-similar—an ordered poise.

The snowflake processes imitate,
    with every falling whole,
a diffused, mirrored forest
    of every branch and bole:
self-cloning—this white noise.

The snowflake processes imitate,
    with every falling whole,
a diffused, mirrored forest
    of every branch and bole:
self-cloning—this white noise.

The crystalline structures step,
    soldiers in perfect rule,
down to the vanishing point
    of any metallic molecule:
self-similar—an ordered poise.

The Pattern

Imperfect memory: snowflakes
creating themselves in their own image
never get it exactly right.
So what you end up with are all these
pleasant approximations: this many points,
that much filigree betwixt,
but no matched pairs. The same
with leaves, their veins and serrate edges.
The same with smoke: the wisps
from twenty identical
votive candles at the shrine
are not identical; they remember only
a general way of rising, curling,
fading. What do you want?
Patterns that make you utter
surprise—nonlinear
plots, fractal
repetitions, Mandelbrot sets,
a template
in the chaotic
penetralia. A winter-white
landscape, its perfect
peace. Woodfires
coiling smoke up the chimney
this year, as in all the others.
In the spring, the leaves coming out
fleshy and soft on the branches
as if on cue, no two alike. You want
a miracle that knows its place: when to be
explicable, and when (your daughter
first stretching her mouth into a grin
you recognize as yours)
an utter surprise.

RITA DOVE

Geometry

I prove a theorem and the house expands:
the windows jerk free to hover near the ceiling,
the ceiling floats away with a sigh.

As the walls clear themselves of everything
but transparency, the scent of carnations
leaves with them. I am out in the open

and above the windows have hinged into butterflies,
sunlight glinting where they've intersected.
They are going to some point true and unproven.

M. C. *Escher's* Circle Limit III

This tessellated hyperbolic plane
is definitely non-Euclidean,
though inside, not on, its circumference
points correspond. Outside is emptiness.

The fish swim back and forth but cannot sense
how they progressively grow small or large
by distance from the unreachable edge
where hypercycles shrink to nothingness.

Thus miracled infinity is viewed,
but only by a god of finitude.

JONATHAN HOLDEN

After Closing Luigi Cremona's Projective Geometry

I don't know how the clouds out here
survived. Points are so perfect that
if you believe in them enough
they prick. Each point will leave
a tiny bruise. And lines are sharp.
The pure ones cut you like the starched
edges of grass-blades, it smarts,
though the wound's too fine to see.
In bristles, they can nearly chafe you
raw. Even here, outdoors, as I stagger
and blink, swamped in this hot mess
of light and sticky shadow, that black
and white headache won't go away.
The points cling in stains, I can't
get rid of them. The vestige
of a line is running furtively along
the street. And the letter *A prime*
still glows in the midst of the elm
tree, while the Principle of Duality
has just flown up and alighted
with those sparrows on the wires.
I can hardly walk, it's underwater,
it's all a jungle here. The leaves flash
their bellies, swimming and wriggling
along in unison, they gobble everything.
The best-trimmed lawns glitter
with chaos like smashed glass. The light's
like acid. You can feel it working
mildly on your skin. The more acid
in the light the more I like it.
I'm going to take a bath in it, splash
this stuff up into my eyes and rub
until the swelling goes away,

then dive in over my head and soak
myself for as long as it takes
to make the dazzle of the last hard
point dissolve in space.

Drawing the Triangle

I reserve the triangle
For the wee hours,
The chigger-sized hours.

I like how it starts out
And never gets there.
I like how it starts out.

In the meantime, the bedroom window
Reflecting the owlish aspect
Of the face and the interior.

One hopes for tangents
Surreptitiously in attendance
Despite the rigors of the absolute.

WILLIAM BRONK

On Divers Geometries

Euclid, Riemann, other geometers,
invented ideas of space. Regarding them,
elation astonishes us: discreteness, shape,
the measure of distances, as though the world
had order in it which were discoverable.
But hardly so; their order is not the world's,
their separately premised spaces not congruent,
as though, besides their spaces, there were space,
not spoken of, unspeakable.

Geometers, all measures measure themselves,
none measures the world. Premise and axiom
are terms of the limited case, to limit it.
There is no limited truth: there is no truth.

JONATHAN HOLDEN

Zeno's Paradox

That absence of imagination sprang
from fear which for years let any man
who swung an axe do the impossible—
clobber the log he aimed at every time.
Even though the axe-head had always
half the distance to the log to go,
it would negotiate this space,
manage somehow to flatten the packed
differentials that remained. It was
a wonder a body could walk across
his room and touch the wall when,
logically, a moving arrow didn't move
at all. But because we're a little
braver than Zeno was, we now know why:
We can face infinity.
When I start out upon this sunlit
floor to cross the room, I'll never
fail. With each stride I take
I perform a commonplace—straddle
the infinite—I cross the infinite
to reach the kitchen wall.

Pure Mathematics

I have been told it is all theory in the end, no letter
    applying to a number
That stands for a thing, no principal accruing interest
    in a practical account,
Only the pure joy of theory and the theory of theories
    I heard
My drunk mathematician friend try to explain one night
    in a Country & Western bar,
Collaring the few who'd listen, truckdrivers and ex-jocks,
    to show them sure proof
That followed some premise they didn't care to understand.

We might have been crabs comprehending opera or sibyls
    poking the blue entrails of frogs,
And still his logic accumulated napkins in an orderly pile
    that the red-haired waitress,
Who finally asked him to leave, swept away and dumped
    under the counter in a barrel.
And driving home later on that icy farm-to-market road,
    he was still
Expounding, jubilantly, maniacally, as the way weaved
    and the universal values
Of arbitrary points unrolled an infinitely expanding line.

It was the clean relish of his mind that made me forget
    the hard curves, the trees
That loomed from the snowy shoulders down to the creek.
    My mind was never like that.
What I liked best the year I studied calculus was chance
    error, my lame prayer
That I might arrive like Columbus, who came by wrong
    to the right unknown. Nothing applied.
O hypothetical mind, we many who are left behind know
    we can never know. We
Stand grounded under the twin wings of the infinite sign.

But in the banking offices near the train station in Rome
    where the currency
Is exchanged—kroners for deutschemarks, yen for lire—
    it all applies.
A button is pushed and the great curve flashes onscreen,
    reckoning all commodities,
All livestock, grains and ores, all modes of production,
    all strikes against management.
And all mismanagement, all mines, ships, wells, and guns
    represent and are represented by
The fluctuation of that curve against the undeviating line

That neither gold, nor oil, nor missiles banked in silos
    will ever turn to theory.
In one of the white lies that numbers tell, I stood there
    while the dollar went
Down on its knees and prayed to the Allah of the Saudis
    and the Buddha of the Japanese
To rise changed into millions of lire, to sing in the grotto
    of the vendor's palm,
O wherever I went all that day, not knowing the language,
    and no difference too
Small, no knowledge that would not be turned to advantage.

11
Biography

Who would put the flesh around this skeleton of facts? . . .

PAUL ZIMMER

JACQUELINE OSHEROW

Somebody Ought to Write a Poem for Ptolemy

Somebody ought to write a poem for Ptolemy,
So ingenious in being wrong, he was almost a poet.
Can anyone follow his configurations?
How he cut a tortured path for every planet
Until his numbers matched what he could see,
Every one spectacularly wrong.
You would think, in all those years of calculations,
He would, at least, have suspected a simpler way.
Maybe he even knew it all along—
The stationary sun, ellipses, everything—
But kept it to himself as too unseemly
Or to save his pregnant wife from all that spinning
And wait beside her in a quiet place
That he, himself, had rendered motionless.

Copernicus

What, then, of Ptolemy
and the favored strands
on his Alexandrine head?
So many burned
in the heretic nightlife

for his errors. He made
the world the center
of the universe,
gave us an envelope
of fixed stars, a slight
miscalculation.

What use was there
in an endless cosmos,
so much space without air,
what possibility of life
beyond the warm green
Mediterranean?

For the Popes,
God lived beyond
the planets and suns,
just behind the black curtain,
the defective evening.

Galileo saw motion
where God should have been.
Two years of house arrest
and what could Galileo say
about it? *It turns.*

PAUL ZIMMER

Notes Toward a Biography of Christiaan Radius,
Near-Sighted Astronomer

Radius, Christiaan Ole (rǎ′ dě ŏos). 1528–1594.
Born to Jorgen and Karen in the hamlet
of Helsingor, where midwives pruned him
By bloody light of the sword-tailed comet
Which had induced his mother's labor.

Apprenticed to a Slesvig glazier,
He learned to grind his lenses
On the bottom of his master's bottles.
Then, in his nineteenth year,
He took an ax up to his attic room
And chopped his future through the roof.

He counted a hundred stars
With his home made alidades,
And swore he'd charted heaven
From God's throne out to its gates.
He called an eclipse fifty times,
But the troll sun disobeyed him,
Being but a tunnel plumb to hell,
Or so he said.

One could say he spent his lifetime
Proving that the world was triangular
In shape, that there were wingèd mice
Upon the moon, that stars were
Shavings from the sun.

One could say that when he died
He had a vision that the comets
Rang like silver gongs in tribute
To his careful scrutiny.

But this biography, no doubt,
Will not be written,

As who would put the flesh
Around this skeleton of facts?
A man is not remembered
For his terrible misjudgements,
No matter how much innocence
He mixes with his ignorance.

CHARLES SIMIC

Dear Isaac Newton

FOR MICHAEL CUDDIHY

Your famous apple
Is still falling.

Your red, ripe,
Properly notarized
Old Testament apple.

(The night's denseness is no help.)

All that we expostulated
To cause her to stay up there.

All the spells and curses
To hold and bind,
To enchant permanently
In the realm of seraphim.

She appeared to dilly dally, to consider.
She was already empyreal,
Ruled by some other reckoning,
When she shuddered and fell.

(The famous *malus pumila*.)

How heavy, how grave she grows
With each headlong instant
As though the seeds inside her
Were a catch of celestial razor-chips.

(Is she suffering for us, Isaac,
In some still incomprehensible way?)

Soon she'll rest at our feet.
Soon she'll strike the earth angrily,

For the earth's a pool table
The gravediggers have hewn with their spades.

Quickly then!
Make your bed,
Set your pillow on the apple
While she still spins.

Understand coldly
Impartially,
There's time only
For a single thought,

A single conjecture
As the bones rejoice in the earth,
As the maggots romp
In the Sunday roast . . .

(The famous apple up there.)

O she's falling lawfully,
But isn't she now
Perhaps even more mysterious
Than when she first started?

And wasn't that one of her
Prize worms
We saw crawling off
Into the unthinkable?

EMILY GROSHOLZ

The Dissolution of the Rainbow

> *By an extraordinary combination of circumstances, the theory of*
> *colors has been drawn into the province and before the tribunal of the*
> *mathematician, a tribunal to which it cannot be said to be amenable.*
>   Goethe, *The Theory of Colors*

A cut-glass chandelier dangled above
the desk where Newton read and wrote;
all morning spectral dragons fought,
mocked him and made love
across the white wall opposite,
flashed their blue and sea-green scales, the fur
of tiny fires, a glittering red eyelight.
Then one day they suddenly
fled, and no longer were.

Rising in impatience, strangely lit
by reason, the philosopher undid
prism by prism the trembling chandelier
to run her now constrained and broken
offspring through a maze of barriers.
The light went through its paces
but the dragons disappeared.
What remained Sir Isaac quantified,
teaching Nature not to sing
her sweeter variations, but in one
low tone, geometry, to answer him.

Although white light is manifold,
a mixture, so he found, of different rays,
each ray could be identified
in essence with its angle of refraction;
this was the only origin of colors,
color then reduced to numbering.
The dragons lapsed to silence, mortified,

curled up and dry as worms a child
has questioned in the fire
of curiosity and left behind.

When Newton set his prism work aside,
he wiped his hands, and wrote on creamy paper
long and elegant formulae,
a shadow of the sensuous retained
in his illuminating study,
even that much immaterial.
Yet he sometimes noticed, later on,
how his sines and cosines lay
across the paper like dark skeletons
of dragon, couchant, rampant as the full
proud curve of the integral.

JENNIFER CLEMENT

William Herschel's Sister, Caroline, Discovers Eight Comets

All in the Fahrenheit of my pulse.

I feel the dust tails,
hear them rustle
in my fringed sleeves.
Shaped like F clefs,
rib-stitched,
I have found the new lights.

On cloud-white evenings
I draw fish hooks,
draw the eye, shank, gap,
throat, bend, barb, point
and polish the telescope,
rest my eyes. Wait.

Whatever
the sky gives me
I will take.

ROSANN KOZLOWSKI

Still the Same

FOR M. CURIE

Marie, that photograph of you at Solvay: simple black dress and gray
hair spun as tight as your lips—the one where you are intently reading
    with Albert,

black suits and mustaches surrounding—not much has changed.
Should it be taken lightly, as scenes from *The Uncertainty Heisenberg*
    Brought to Life?

The Terror of Thermodynamics? The Horrible Hamiltonians? You could have
made a B-rated film image yourself. I believe they called you Madame

because they couldn't comprehend who would stir pots of uranium as
    morning
filtered through the window, hands chapped clean by the process
    you penned.

When I visited your homeland and touched the cold bronze plaque, I
wanted to steal it. I did. Tuck it in my bag, take it home, curl up next to it,

the alchemy cool against my skin. Who would notice it gone? You
received more publicity for an affair than for the elements
    you extracted or the prizes Nobel

had sent. So when you wrote that you could not live without the
    laboratory,
I laughed. Not the husband long gone or the daughters,
    but that room

with the molten stew that made you. Then beat you. And your
shoulders would square, throwing that intense radioactive stare.

MICHAEL L. JOHNSON

Roentgen

Voltage turned all the way up,
he waits until his eyes work
in the dark, then holds his hand
between the glass discharge tube
and a small fluorescent screen:
faint bone shadows in that glow,
the body's science become
at once deep and colorless.

Ludwig Boltzmann

The bust above his tomb in Vienna displays
the brow that built the formula engraved
below: entropy is proportional,

by way of his constant, to the logarithm
of the probability of a given state.
Though law bends stars like slaves, order degrades.

Messes get messier, like a child's room—
unless someone picks things up and vacuums.
Life counters chaos; still, warm air tends to cool.

This difficult and charming man could fill
the lecture halls of Europe when he explained
the thermodynamics of theoretic atoms.

But all systems run down, and his thought came
to seem too mechanical, he a throwback
Maxwell's demon would never let through the gate.

Most of his life he suffered from manic
depression, asthma, then angina, headaches.
Einstein might have helped, had there been time.

Vacationing at Duino, while his wife
and daughter swam in the Adriatic,
he stayed in the hotel room and hanged himself.

JENNIFER CLEMENT

Einstein Thinks about the Daughter He Put Up for Adoption and Then Could Never Find

Perhaps
She uses her fingers
like a compass
making circles in the dirt.

Perhaps
she cuts her hand
in the dark day,
splitting an atom
in the middle of her palm.

Particles of light curve
through glass-empty windows.

Numbers tattooed on her wrist
are blue equations,
and the knots in the barbed wire
look like stars.

He hugs his violin—
small body of wood.

BIN RAMKE

The Monkish Mind of the Speculative Physicist

A wisp of slight sound, an echo of an echo
through the trees—or something imaginary
    projected by

his fevered brain. Bilaniuk examined long
into the night the properties of
    imaginary mass:

according to Relativity Theory he found
that at one and a half times the speed
    of light a rock

which weighed in this world a pound would weigh
the square-root-of-minus-one pounds.
    The number is called

Imaginary, not impossible, and if, he said,
a particle could go so fast it would only
    slow down

the more it was pushed. An Adam who conjured
new creatures to name, he called them
    Tachyons. A slight

fever was the cause, and insomnia, nothing
really, just the influenza then in fashion.
    A dripping faucet,

a lack of stillness in the night becomes
a dread and catches on the tick of the clock
    as annoyingly

as silk on a hangnail. Meanwhile a woman
emerged into morning from a night
    of bad dreams.

She wandered into the small garden
and tried not to think of the children
    still sleeping

or the husband oblivious in bed. She watched
sunlight slice itself in the dew of an iris,
   considered how

it might be in a fair foreign country to live
with a dark stranger. She is frightened
   of her mirroring mind

   reflecting what never was
onto what cannot be, nameless, forever:
a wisp of slight sound, an echo of an echo.

MICHAEL L. JOHNSON

At the Cavendish Laboratory, 1941

after Chadwick
checked the math

and knew how
small a mass

of uranium
could go

critical
he already saw

too much
of the future

but had no one
to talk to

his colleagues
foreigners now

more than ever
sleepless

he took pills
each night

for the rest
of his life

ROALD HOFFMANN

Fritz Haber

invented a catalyst to mine cubic miles
of nitrogen from air. He fixed the gas
with iron chips; German factories coming
on stream, pouring out tons of ammonia,

fertilizers, months before the sea-lines
to Chilean saltpeter and guano were cut,
just in time to stock powder, explosives
for the Great War. Haber knew how catalysts

work, that a catalyst is not innocent, but
joins in, to carve off the top or undermine
some critical hill, or, reaching molecular
arms for the partners in the most difficult

stage of reaction, brings them near, eases
the desired making and breaking of bonds.
The catalyst, reborn, rises to its match-
making again; a cheap pound of Haber's

primped iron could make a million pounds
of ammonia. Geheimrat Haber of the Kaiser
Wilhelm Institute thought himself a catalyst
for ending the War; his chemical weapons

would bring victory in the trenches; burns
and lung cankers were better than a dum-dum
bullet, shrapnel. When his men unscrewed
the chlorine tank caps and green gas spilled

over the dawn field at Ypres he carefully
took notes, forgot his wife's sad letters.
After the War Fritz Haber dreamed in Berlin
of mercury and sulfur, the alchemists' work

hastening the world, changing themselves.
He wondered how he could extract the millions

of atoms of gold in every liter of water,
transmuting the sea to the stacked bullion

of the German war debt. And the world, well,
it *was* changing; in Munich one could hear
the boots of brown-shirted troopers, one paid
a billion marks for lunch. A catalyst again,

that's what he would find, and found—himself,
in Basel, the foreign town on the banks of his
Rhine, there he found himself, the Protestant
Geheimrat Haber, now the Jew Haber, in the city
of wily Paracelsus, a changed and dying man.

JOHN WITTE

Robert Oppenheimer, 1945

The sky seethes and shifts: you yourself
change in the dark, rain lashing, a blinding flash

illuminating the tower at Zero, the bomb
in its cradle (*"this object*
might go off accidently!"). You gave it a name: *Trinity*,
after Donne's holy sonnet, "Batter my heart, three person'd God."

Four packs a day, you gasp, galumphing
flatfooted, 115 pounds on a six-foot frame, enchiladas
and chile peppers *burning you up inside.* Torn
between fear of the Gadget
failing, and fear that it won't, you electrify
your congregation of scientists and engineers: *his poetic vision*
inflames me. I feel more intelligent, more prescient,
more poetic myself. The flesh
blistering, you quote
Baudelaire (*Fleurs du Mal*). You hate this world, ·
this body. You hate your children, casting them off, offering
the baby to friends for adoption. You give everything a new name,

"top" (for atom), "boat" (for bomb),
"topic boat" (atom bomb), and "tickling the tail of the dragon"
(with a screwdriver, inching two lumps of plutonium
together to the *point of criticality*). Your secret
community assembling
the steel tower girder by girder
100 feet over the desert, at the top a corrugated metal shack
open to the camera bunker 5 miles west—*our life here*
is directed. . . . It is as though we are programmed
to do one thing—a winch
hoisting the five-ton sphere into place,
the coded message sent out: "Baby due to arrive July 16."

Gaunt, slumped,
checking the seismographs and oscilloscopes, the galvanometers,
ionization chambers, geophones and spectrographs,

you thumb a Sanskrit
Bhagavad-Gita: *If the radiance*
of a thousand suns were to burst at once into the sky,
that would be like the splendor of the Mighty One . . . I am become
Death, shatterer of worlds.

The clouds part; a star
appears. A toad emerges from the sand
and begins its low-pitched, raspy bleating. You remember it
from your boyhood—
the sand, mesquite and Mariposa lilies,
the space immense, and transparently clear: void of human life.
Coddled, an "unctuous, repulsively good little boy,"
you were sent here to heal
your lungs, camping and chopping wood, riding
through lush upland meadows, flowers brushing the horse's loins,
then down across the desert, peach and lavender, riding
the Jornada del Muerto to Los Alamos. *My childhood . . .*
gave me no normal, healthy way to be a bastard.

A loud crumping near the tower,
you shine your light on a puddle
crowded with toads, their throats ballooning, each so intent
on his song a female must
nudge him
to tell him she is there,
willing, swollen with unlaid eggs.

You climb the ladder,
the bomb crouched in a thicket of cables, switches
and detonators, deep in its core the plug of beryllium, penile,
hot with polonium alphas. You touch the metal skin: *live,*
like a rabbit. You return to the bunker,
waxen, cadaverous, whispering
" . . . the enterprise . . . so macabre." Goggle-eyed,
you curl like a fetus on the floor.

The cameras begin to churn.

BRUCE BERGER

Murray

What of those who abandon their weight to chairs
Full knowing you can't simultaneously fix
A particle's motion and place: who keep their balance
Buttressed by flesh revealed to be a chance
Averaging of events that can't be assured;
Informed that possibly massless particles
Pommel the most Nobeled cerebral cortex
Finding nobody at home; those, that is,
For whom this headlong cosmos fanned and thinned
From the tiniest asymmetries way back when,
And will keep on thinning into oblivion
Until more matter shows up; who find their own
Curiosity a most curious occurrence,
Mere pattern chasing pattern, pooled ambition
Storming that reclusive elegance,
The simplest way to corner the complex?
What if you were the man who posited quarks?

He travels around the globe looking at birds.
His lifelist corners half the surviving species
While, en route, he annexes the world's
Tales to date, its politics, its jokes,
Its sauces, its diseases, its interiors,
Its braided languages and its unraveling
Habitats, for which he contrives some grants.
The world, in turn, extends its elegance
In the form of his favorite bird, the elegant trogon:
Each year, come spring, he joins an unpredictable
Mass of fellow birders at the South Fork
Of Cave Creek, where the bird preens its iridescence
On the campground john, casually scattering photons
Into the magnification of paired ground lenses
That jam its fire into the rods and cones
Of awestruck eyes, while whispering into the whorls
Of Murray's all-deciphering ears, *quark, quark* . . .

MICHAEL L. JOHNSON

Stephen Hawking Oraculates

FOR DAN

> . . . *the aequiuocation which is as bottomlesse as the pit of hell.* . . .
> Thomas Morton

The room quiet as an adytum, class begins.

Seated in his wheelchair, paralyzed, skeletal,
the teacher speaks in a wavering, broken drone
of the first instants of the universe, the chant
incoherent except to his interpreter,
who, standing at the blackboard, draws a circular
manifold. All that telescopes watch in the sky
happened in the past. One imagines mastodons
grazing Central Park, but this is more difficult.

Students ask questions. After each, the drone resumes,
chthonic. Space is mostly emptiness twisted by
gravity. Once it was perfect symmetry—till
some plenipotent particle appeared. Perhaps
there was no origin, so time blooms anew now,
now. Horizons may be only metaphors, what
nerves do. Can protons decay? Think about these things.

The drone stops. Silence echoes, inflating the room
like an abyss. The Pythian is rolled away.

BIN RAMKE

The Astronomer Works Nights: A Parable of Science

> *Lobachevsky . . . and Bolyai . . . first asserted and proved*
> *that the axiom of parallels is not necessarily true.*
>   H. P. Manning

> *Opusculum paedogogum. / The pears are not viols*
>   Wallace Stevens

What else in this dark world turns true?
Three pears and an apple in the bowl
on my table near the charts, dust,
the memory of silver stars, and breakfast.
Stars pop

like corn on a griddle if you watch them
as I do. The greatest calamities
the universe has known make no sound
like the deadliest trees in the forest.
Stars leave eggs under the fingernails
while you sleep.

I look at points and I make lines
to link stars in sleep which comes
with the sun. I have never touched
what alone I love, which is the light
which is clean and cold
as I am.

My wife and daughter loved me before
my skin grew translucent as a lampshade;
I can see stars through it when I hold
my hand against the night.

★   ★   ★

What I *do* is photograph
a section of the sky

smaller than the last
segment of the orange
after you took a bite.
Then I measure
the negatives.

While a student twenty
years ago I walked
the wet brick paths
on cooling afternoons;
I listened to the sky
crack as heat escaped;
I would not eat for days
because I liked
the strange dark feeling
(or sometimes half
an orange, closely peeled).

★　★　★

The bones glow white as stars
hidden in the map of flesh
and the universe laughs quietly
just over some dark ridge.

Perhaps I *can* hear it
ticking like an engine block
cooling on the side of the road
while adulterers walk
arm in arm in the woods.

Slow Hercules stalks Cygnus
and the Dragon insinuates between:
some nights I see it all come true;

I am the cosmic peeping Tom,
and what intimacies I spy on
through stars like wistful windows

while beauty lies sadly
with the world.

But when I wander home and hear
a wife and lover laughing in the shadows
I wonder whether some night I might watch
a dance much closer if not more slow;

our final hope is that we will not know.

JANE SHORE

An Astronomer's Journal

Even in sleep my eyes are on the elements.
My eyes are pencils being perpetually resharpened
puzzling out the sky's connecting dots
one almost expects to be accompanied by numbers,
jig-saw animal-shaped constellations,
bear, bent dipper, wed fish in repose,
crowding out the angels who I suppose
must be stacked up tier on tier
as in the horseshoe of the opera house.
Each night the sky splits open like a melon
its starry filaments
the astronomer examines with great intensity.
Caught in his expensive glass eye
more microscope than telescope,
it is his own eye he sees, reflected
and possessed, a moon-disc in a lake,
safe, even to himself, untouchable;
and so his notion of himself must be corrected:
"Actually, the universe is introspective."

MARTHA HOLLANDER

The Archaeologist's Dream

Pain, like a diamond,
can slice through anything,
has a thousand sharp aspects.
I'm a boy of seven again, running,
falling headlong on smooth concrete
and breaking a tooth. I can see
the alien white piece lying there
like bone china destroyed in a rage,
now part of the world's random scatterings.
Stunned by this new absence, I don't even
examine or preserve the brittle bit
the way a sick person coos over
his sore extremities. Instead
I leave it to be lost
in a confusion of children,
trampled and driven underfoot
by decades of small sturdy shoes.
Teeth are the proudest of our ornaments.
It was a front one that broke, and so
history can be read in the small flaw
just as I can read it in pottery sherds,
in the grave, chipped faces of statues.
Teeth urge us to bite as we kiss.
It's many years later, and I am kissed,
it appears, by a woman who eagerly
grasps the nature of artifacts.
She knows something is missing
as she digs in my mouth with her own.
I know she is hunting for that fragment,
for what I'd buried so much earlier,
and her breathless excavation will
bring her what she wants.
My own work on a distant hill unearthed

a few black pebbles, elegantly concave,
that turned out to be ancient garlic.
I bit one, more a challenge than a joke,
and the resonance of the old break
suddenly soared along my jaw. It was
as if that equivocal little rock
would absorb me into its impossible age.
I can feel it now as she hits,
like a pulsing nerve of gold, pay dirt.
She cradles the fragment in the hot
intelligence of her hands, holds it
up to the light, dusts it off,
and laughs aloud at the discovery.
And again the great negative space
invades who I am, shattering my face
into a thousand sharp aspects,
slicing through all of me,
like a diamond, pain.

EMILY GROSHOLZ

Reflections on the Transfinite

Reading about the tower or great-boled tree
of ordinals, I think how Cantor grew
more wise and more insane, trying to save
his tree of Jesse from the pruning shears
and kitchen gardening of Kronecker;
though I must share the latter's feeling for
the natural numbers, those deceptively
well-ordered, step-wise creatures, which appear
transparent as they mount, but all in all
among themselves are most unknowable.

Dreaming about the cardinals, at night,
the alephs flaming like a candelabrum,
I see you in the attic of your house
installed between Diogenes Laertius,
nachgelassene Schriften, commentary
on Aristotle, Plato, and the latest
fashionable fact-shredders out of Paris.
So cloudy is the place you occupy
in the last hierarchies of my world
that I hardly discern you; yet I know
you are not just a postulate I made.

You are the great collection of desires,
forever incomplete, unsatisfied,
toward which all finite sequences in time
with little steps so trustfully aspire.
Though you outrank them all, see how they run
like atomies of fire toward the sun,
sent over the abyss with no alarm
to make the leap across into your arms.

JONATHAN HOLDEN

The Fall of Pythagoras

Once all his calculations came out
like peas. You could pop them
whole from the pod, perfect spheres.
And they were sweet. The number two
tasted the way deep fields taste
after rain. You could take the trees
apart, find godlike shapes
if you didn't look too hard,
which is why I feel sorry for
Pythagoras. He tried to take a pure
square apart, he was tinkering
around too much. One hard look
at the diagonal, and it was too
late. The quality of light
had already changed. It lent the wind
forbidden possibilities, the clouds
this odd, this brooding weight;
for the diagonal was the square root
of Two. And what Two was made of—
this hard, sweet pea—what all
these leaves, these animals and clouds,
the sun, even these ugly dreams
he'd been having recently at night
were made of, would not add up.
The harder you tried to add them
up, the finer they became, the faster
sifted through your fingers
the incommensurable parts of everything.

JONATHAN HOLDEN

Ramanujan

> *It was Mr. Littlewood (I believe) who remarked that "every
> positive integer was one of his [Ramanujan's] personal friends."*
>   G. H. Hardy

This modest, mousy little boy from India
could reel off pi's digits to any
decimal place his classmates dared him to.
No mean feat. But for Ramanujan it
was a breeze. Pi was merely one of his
first cousins, in fact a favorite.
And his cousins were innumerable.
Each day when school let out he'd retire
to the silent playground where they waited,
a windless plot with neither sun nor moon.
A silent playground—it was a funny place,
part civilized and partly wilderness.
It had some cultivated sections, but
all the rows, like footprints in the snow,
simply petered out into a white
fastness that was neither far nor near.
There was no definite horizon there.

Without a word, Ramanujan would sit
down among his friends and question them.
Some were persnickety at first, but if
he scattered seed and sat still long
enough, they'd hop right up to him.
Like sparrows, they'd eat out of his hand.
And once a number had confessed, Ramanujan
was its intimate. Each face touched off
for him its sly Gestalt, it pulled the trigger
that the kindly puss of your old car pulls
as you pick it out among the traffic,
idling with its crotchety click-click,

it was the smell of home cooking.
When Hardy once casually remarked
that the integer one seven two nine
on a taxi seemed "quite dull," Ramanujan
quickened. Why no, it was the smallest sum
of two cubes expressible in just two ways.

When he died, his room was packed. The walls,
the clock, the close air bristled with his friends.
As he expired, softly they slipped off,
those countless cousins, all without a word,
without jostling a single speck of dust,
without leaving the slightest trace behind,
without touching anything, fled back
to haunt that playground where for thirty years
he'd shuffled out and sat. The rest of us,
still stuck here in the shambles, go right on
sneezing with the seasons and galumph around
grabbing the daffodils too hard, bruising
the fruit, ordering the weeds to state their names,
waiting for the scent after the thunderstorm,
the shot, the drenching accident, to be
the Ramanujans of experience.

IRA SADOFF

The Mathematician's Disclaimer

What I would give for a clear field
of vision, to rid myself of the crippling
disorder of my desk, my only child
standing before my wife, the wild
grass growing slowly over my shoetops.
I have given my life to numbers, and these
numbers, in return, have given me a life
I cannot control. But that is all
beside the point. Nothing is really solved:
as the photograph resolves in its pan,
the plan to map the path of the sun
cannot be won. What a relief to know
that if my days are numbered I have numbered
them myself, the pleasure in the music
of my life is not left in the clock, nor
the tock of the metronome, but in the moment
between moments, the measure left unmeasured.

Acknowledgments

Aisenberg, Nadya. "Measures." *Poetry* (June 1996): 125. Copyright © 1996 by Modern Poetry Association. Reprinted with permission from the editor of *Poetry* and the author.

Aisenberg, Nadya. "Sum." Copyright © 1998 by Nadya Aisenberg. Printed with permission from the author.

Ammons, A. R. "Prodigal," "Mechanism," "Identity," "Expressions of Sea Level," "Saliences," and "Cascadilla Falls." In *The Selected Poems of A. R. Ammons*. New York: W. W. Norton, 1987, 19–20, 21–22, 27–29, 35–37, 47–50, 62. Copyright © 1987, 1977, 1975, 1974, 1972, 1971, 1970, 1966, 1965, 1964, 1955 by A. R. Ammons. Reprinted with permission from W. W. Norton and Company, Inc.

Antler. "On Learning on the Clearest Night Only 6000 Stars Are Visible to the Naked Eye." In *A Second Before It Bursts*. Milwaukee, Wisc.: Woodland Pattern Book Center, 1994. Copyright © 1994 by Antler. Reprinted with permission from the author.

Bangs, Carol Jane. "The Poet Studies Physics." In *The Bones of the Earth*. New York: New Directions Publishing Corporation, 1983, 49. Copyright © 1977, 1978, 1983 by Carol Jane Bangs. Reprinted with permission from New Directions Publishing Corporation.

Berger, Bruce. "Stellar Gothic." *Light* (winter 1996–1997). Copyright © 1997 by Bruce Berger. Reprinted with permission from the author.

Berger, Bruce. "Astrophysicists." *Light* (summer 1992). Copyright © 1992 by Bruce Berger. Reprinted with permission from the author.

Berger, Bruce. "Murray." In *Facing the Music*. Lewiston, Idaho: Confluence Press, 1995, 16. Copyright © 1995 by Bruce Berger. Reprinted with permission from Confluence Press, Lewis-Clark State College, Lewiston, ID 83501–2698.

Berland, Dinah. "All Together, Nothing Lost." Chester H. Jones Foundation National Poetry Competition 1998. Copyright © 1998 by Dinah Berland. Reprinted with permission from the author.

Bronk, William. "Boolean Algebra: $X^2 = X$" and "On Divers Geometries." In *Life Supports: New and Collected Poems*. San Francisco: North Point Press, 1981, 62–63, 101. Copyright © 1981 by William Bronk. Reprinted with permission from the author.

Buckley, Christopher. "Star Journal," "Isotropic," and "Speculation in Dark Air." In *Dark Matter*. Providence, R.I.: Copper Beach Press, 1993. Copyright © 1993 by Christopher Buckley. Reprinted with permission from the author.

Burns, Ralph. "Stars." In *Mozart's Starling*. Athens: Ohio Review Books, 1990, 28–29. Copyright © 1990 by Ralph Burns. Reprinted with permission from Ohio Review Books.

Clement, Jennifer. "William Herschel's Sister, Caroline, Discovers Eight Comets" and "Einstein Thinks about the Daughter He Put Up for Adoption and Then Could Never Find." Copyright © 1998 by Jennifer Clement. Printed with permission from the author.

Collier, Michael. "The Heavy Light of Shifting Stars." In *The Folded Heart*. Middletown, Conn.: Wesleyan University Press, 1989, 36. Copyright © 1989 by Michael Collier. Reprinted with permission from University Press of New England.

Collins, Billy. "Earthling." In *The Apple That Astonished Paris*. Fayetteville: University of Arkansas Press, 1988, 37. Copyright © 1988 by Billy Collins. Reprinted with permission from University of Arkansas Press.

Deming, Alison Hawthorne. "Mt. Lemmon, Steward Observatory, 1990" and "The Woman Painting Crates." In *Science and Other Poems*. Baton Rouge: Louisiana State University Press, 1994, 53–56, 58–59. Copyright © 1994 by Alison Hawthorne Deming. Reprinted with permission from Louisiana State University Press.

Deming, Alison Hawthorne. "Genetic Sequence" (originally titled "26"), "Essay on Intelligence: One," "Essay on Intelligence: Two," "Essay on Intelligence: Three," "Essay on Intelligence: Four," "Essay on Intelligence: Five," "Essay on Intelligence: Six," and "Essay on Intelligence: Seven." In *The Monarchs*. Baton Rouge: Louisiana State University Press, 1997, 32, 21, 29–30, 34–35, 46, 48, 54, 62. Copyright © 1997 by Alison Hawthorne Deming. Reprinted with permission from Louisiana State University Press.

Dennis, Carl. "The Anthropic Cosmological Principle" and "Evolution." In *Meetings with Time*. New York: Penguin Books, 1992, 23–24, 47–48. Copyright © 1992 by Carl Dennis. Reprinted with permission from Viking Penguin, a division of Penguin Books USA, Inc.

Der-Hovanessian, Diana. "Fractals." *American Scholar* (summer 1989). Copyright © 1989 by Diana Der-Hovanessian. Reprinted with permission from the author.

Dillingham, Peter. "Black Holes & Hologramarye." In *POLY: New Speculative Writing*. Mountain View, Calif.: Ocean View Books, 1989. Copyright © 1989 by Peter Dillingham. Reprinted with permission from the author.

Dove, Rita. "The Fish in the Stone." In *Museum*. Pittsburgh, Pa.: Carnegie Mellon University Press, 1983, 13. Copyright © 1983 by Rita Dove. Reprinted with permission from the author.

Dove, Rita. "Geometry." In *The Yellow House on the Corner*. Pittsburgh, Pa.: Carnegie Mellon University Press, 1989, 21. Copyright © 1980 by Rita Dove. Reprinted with permission from the author.

Duhamel, Denise. "The Future of Vaginas and Penises." In *Girl Soldier*. Truro, Mass.: Garden Street Press, 1996, 61. Copyright © 1996 by Denise Duhamel. Reprinted with permission from Garden Street Press, P.O. 1231, Truro, MA 02666–1231.

Duhamel, Denise. "Facing My Amygdala." Copyright © 1998 by Denise Duhamel. Printed with permission from the author.

Eiseley, Loren. "Notes of an Alchemist." In *Notes of an Alchemist*. New York: Charles Scribner's Sons, 1972, 15–17. Copyright © 1972 by Loren Eiseley. Reprinted with permission from Scribner, a division of Simon and Schuster, Inc.

Feinfeld, D. A. "Sea Lilies" and "Skeleton Key." Copyright © 1998 by D. A. Feinfeld. Printed with permission from the author.

Francis, Robert. "Astronomer" and "Comet." In *Robert Francis: Collected Poems 1936–1976*. Amherst: University of Massachusetts Press, 1976. Copyright © 1976 by Robert Francis. Reprinted with permission from University of Massachusetts Press.

Frazier, Robert. "A Fractal Pattern." In *POLY: New Speculative Writing*. Mountain View, Calif.: Ocean View Books, 1989. Copyright © 1989 by Robert Frazier. Reprinted with permission from the author.

Gander, Forrest. "Time and the Hour." In *Science and Steepleflower*. New York: New Directions Publishing Corporation, 1998. Copyright © 1998 by Forrest Gander. Reprinted with permission from the author.

Goldbarth, Albert. "Farder to Reache." *Ohio Review* 47 (1991). Copyright © 1991 by Albert Goldbarth. Reprinted with permission from the author.

Goldbarth, Albert. "Tarpan and Aurochs" and "Vestigial." In *Arts and Sciences*. Princeton, N.J.: Ontario Review Press, 1986, 3–5, 6–7. Copyright © 1986 by Albert Goldbarth. Reprinted with permission from the author.

Goldbarth, Albert. "Reality Organization" and "The Sciences Sing a Lullabye." In *Heaven and Earth*. Athens: University of Georgia Press, 1991, 101–103, 118–19. Copyright © 1991 by Albert Goldbarth. Reprinted with permission from University of Georgia Press.

Graham, Jorie. "from Sir Francis Bacon's *Novum Organum.*" In *Materialism*. New York: Ecco Press, 1993, 21–24, 78. Copyright © 1993 by Jorie Graham. Reprinted with permission from The Ecco Press.

Greenberg, Alvin. "c = the physics of farewell." In *heavy wings*. Athens: Ohio Review Books, 1988, 29. Copyright © 1988 by Alvin Greenberg. Reprinted with permission from Ohio Review Books.

Grosholz, Emily. "Poems Overheard at a Conference on Relativity Theory" and "Rivers." Copyright © 1998 by Emily Grosholz. Reprinted with permission from the author.

Grosholz, Emily. "The Dissolution of the Rainbow" and "Reflections on the Transfinite." In *The River Painter*. Urbana: University of Illinois Press, 1984, 67–68, 74. Copyright © 1984 by Emily Grosholz. Reprinted with permission from the author and University of Illinois Press.

Hiestand, Emily. "Os" and "Earth's Answer." Copyright © 1998 by Emily Hiestand. Reprinted with permission from the author. An earlier form of "Earth's Answer" was published in *Carolina Quarterly* 43, no. 3 (spring 1991).

Hiestand, Emily. "On First Reading Particle Physics" (originally titled "Route One"). In *Green the Witch-Hazel Wood*. St. Paul, Minn.: Graywolf Press, 1989, 6. Copyright ©

Ignatow, David. "Poet to Physicist in His Laboratory." In *Figures of the Human.* Middletown, Conn.: Wesleyan University Press, 1964. Copyright © 1964 by David Ignatow. Reprinted with permission from University Press of New England.

Inez, Colette. "Neutrinos." Copyright © 1998 by Colette Inez. Printed with permission from the author.

Inez, Colette. "Seven Stages of Skeletal Decay." In *Getting Under Way: New and Selected Poems.* Brownsville, Oreg.: Story Line Press, 1993, 23–24. Copyright © 1993 by Colette Inez. Reprinted with permission from Story Line Press.

Johanssen, Kerry. "The 9+2 Roseate Anatomy of Microtubules." Copyright © 1998 by Kerry Johanssen. Printed with permission from the author.

Johnson, Michael L. "Fibonacci Time Lines." In *The Unicorn Captured.* Lawrence, Kans.: Cottonwood Review Press, 1980. Copyright © 1980 by Michael L. Johnson. Reprinted with permission from the author.

Johnson, Michael L. "Schrödinger's Cat." *California State Poetry Quarterly* 13, no. 3 (1986). Copyright © 1986 by Michael L. Johnson. Reprinted with permission from the author.

Johnson, Michael L. "M. C. Escher's *Circle Limit III.*" In *Familiar Stranger.* Lawrence, Kans.: Flowerpot Mountain Press, 1983. Copyright © 1983 by Michael L. Johnson. Reprinted with permission from the author.

Johnson, Michael L. "Roentgen." Copyright © 1998 by Michael L. Johnson. Printed with permission from the author.

Johnson, Michael L. "Ludwig Boltzmann." *West* 7 (1992). Copyright © 1992 by Michael L. Johnson. Reprinted with permission from the author.

Johnson, Michael L. "At the Cavendish Laboratory, 1941." *G. W. Review* 11, no. 1 (1990). Copyright © 1990 by Michael L. Johnson. Reprinted with permission from the author.

Johnson, Michael L. "Stephen Hawking Oraculates." *Windless Orchard* 53 (1990). Copyright © 1990 by Michael L. Johnson. Reprinted with permission from the author.

Johnson, Ronald. "Beam 4" and "Beam 7." In *Ark: The Foundations.* San Francisco: North Point Press, 1980. Copyright © 1980 by Ronald Johnson. Reprinted with permission from the author.

Jones, Alice. "The Blood." *Lancet* 349 (March 29, 1997). Copyright © 1997 by Alice Jones. Reprinted with permission from the author.

Jones, Alice. "The Cell" and "The Lungs." *Annals of Internal Medicine* 119, no. 6 (1993). Copyright © 1993 by Alice Jones. Reprinted with permission from the author.

Jones, Alice. "The Inner Ear." *New England Journal of Medicine* 325, no. 9 (1991). Copyright © 1991 by Alice Jones. Reprinted with permission from the author.

Jones, Alice. "The Larynx." *Zyzzyva* 9, no. 1 (spring 1993). Copyright © 1993 by Alice Jones. Reprinted with permission from the author.

Prospere, Susan. "Heavenly Bodies." In *Sub Rosa*. New York: W. W. Norton, 1992, 22–23. Copyright © 1992 by Susan Prospere. Reprinted with permission from W. W. Norton and Company, Inc.

Ramke, Bin. "The Monkish Mind of the Speculative Physicist." In *The Language Student*. Baton Rouge: Louisiana State University Press, 1986, 47–48. Copyright © 1986 by Bin Ramke. Reprinted with permission from Louisiana State University Press.

Ramke, Bin. "The Astronomer Works Nights: A Parable of Science." In *The Difference between Day and Night*. New Haven, Conn.: Yale University Press, 1978, 34–36. Copyright © 1978 by Bin Ramke. Reprinted with permission from Yale University Press.

Revard, Carter. "Earth and Diamonds" and "This Is Your Geode Talking" (previously published as "Geode"). In *An Eagle Nation*. Tucson: University of Arizona Press, 1993, 91–92, 103–106. Copyright © 1993 by Carter Revard. Reprinted with permission from University of Arizona Press.

Roberts, Len. "Learning the Stars." In *Counting the Black Angels*. Urbana: University of Illinois Press, 1994, 94–95. Copyright © 1994 by Len Roberts. Reprinted with permission from the author and University of Illinois Press.

Roberts, Len. "Learning the Planets." In *Dangerous Angels*. Providence, R.I.: Copper Beech Press, 1993, 10–11. Copyright © 1993 by Len Roberts. Reprinted with permission from the author.

Rogers, Pattiann. "The Rites of Passage," "Achieving Perspective," "The Brain Creates Itself," "The Pieces of Heaven," "The Definition of Time," "The Possible Advantages of the Expendable Multitudes," "The Voice of the Precambrian Sea," "The Origin of Order," "Good Heavens," and "Life in an Expanding Universe." In *Firekeeper.* Minneapolis, Minn.: Milkweed Editions, 1994, 20–21, 25–26, 27, 53–54, 69–70, 73–74, 133–34, 135–36, 182–84, 251. Copyright © 1994 by Pattiann Rogers.

Rogers, Pattiann. "Fractal: Repetition of Form over a Variety of Scales." In *Eating Bread and Honey*. Minneapolis, Minn.: Milkweed Editions, 1997, 55–56. Copyright © 1997 by Pattiann Rogers.

Rogers, Pattiann. "Fossil Texts in Canyon Walls." *Weber Studies: An Interdisciplinary Humanities Journal* 14, no. 1 (winter 1997). Copyright © 1997 by Pattiann Rogers. Reprinted with permission from the author.

Rollings, Alane. "About Time" and "Tomorrow Is a Difficult Idea." In *The Struggle to Adore*. Brownsville, Oreg.: Story Line Press, 1994, 59–61, 74–75. Copyright © 1994 by Alane Rollings. Reprinted with permission from Story Line Press.

Rosen, Kenneth. "Amor Fati." Copyright © 1998 by Kenneth Rosen. Printed with permission from the author.

Sadoff, Ira. "The Mathematician's Disclaimer." In *Settling Down*. Boston: Houghton Mifflin, 1975, 17. Copyright © 1975 by Ira Sadoff. Reprinted with permission from the author.

Saner, Reg. "Ploughing the Dark." In *So This Is the Map*. New York: Random House, 1981, 41–42. Copyright © 1981 by Reg Saner. Reprinted with permission from Random House, Inc.

Saner, Reg. "Vespers." In *Essay on Air*. Athens: Ohio Review Books, 1984, 41. Copyright © 1984 by Reg Saner. Reprinted with permission from Ohio Review Books.

Seibles, Tim. "Something Silver-White." In *Hurdy-Gurdy*. Cleveland: Cleveland State University Press, 1992. Copyright © 1992 by Tim Seibles. Reprinted with permission from the author.

Seidel, Frederick. "The New Cosmology." In *These Days*. New York: Alfred A. Knopf, 1989, 10–11. Copyright © 1989 by Frederick Seidel. Reprinted with permission from Alfred A. Knopf, Inc.

Shore, Jane. "An Astronomer's Journal." In *Eye Level*. Amherst: University of Massachusetts Press, 1977, 31. Copyright © 1977 by Jane Shore. Reprinted with permission from University of Massachusetts Press. Originally published in *Poetry*.

Simic, Charles. "Many Zeros." In *Hotel Insomnia*. New York: Harcourt Brace Jovanovich, 1992, 41. Copyright © 1992 by Charles Simic. Reprinted with permission from Harcourt Brace and Company.

Simic, Charles. "Ghost Stories Written." In *The World Doesn't End: Prose Poems*. San Diego: Harcourt Brace, 1989, 13. Copyright © 1989 by Charles Simic. Reprinted with permission from Harcourt Brace and Company.

Simic, Charles. "Madonnas Touched Up with a Goatee," "Drawing the Triangle," and "Dear Isaac Newton." In *Austerities*. New York: George Braziller, 1982, 42, 47, 55–56. Copyright © 1982 by Charles Simic. Reprinted with permission from George Braziller, Inc., and the author.

Sokol, John. "Thoughts near the Close of Millennium." *Quarterly West* 41 (autumn/winter 1995–1996). Copyright © 1995 by John Sokol. Reprinted with permission from the author.

Stafford, William. "On Earth," "What If We Were Alone?" and "Looking Up at Night." In *An Oregon Message*. New York: Harper and Row, Publishers, 1987, 50, 115, 123. Copyright © 1987 by William Stafford. Reprinted with permission from the Estate of William Stafford.

Stanton, Maura. "Computer Map of the Early Universe." *Hopewell Review* 6 (1994). Copyright © 1994 by Maura Stanton. Reprinted with permission from the author.

Strickland, Stephanie. "Presto! How the Universe Is Made." In *True North*. Notre Dame, Ind.: University of Notre Dame Press, 1997, 27. Copyright © 1997 by Stephanie Strickland. Reprinted with permission from University of Notre Dame Press.

Swensen, Cole. "New Math." In *New Math*. New York: William Morrow and Company, 1988, 19. Copyright © 1988 by Cole Swensen. Reprinted with permission from William Morrow and Company.

Swenson, Karen. "Dinosaur National." In *A Sense of Direction*. New York: The Smith, 1989, 33–34. Copyright © 1989 by Karen Swenson. Reprinted with permission from the author.

Sze, Arthur. "The Redshifting Web." In *Archipelago*. Port Townsend, Wash.: Copper Canyon Press, 1995, 45–56. Copyright © 1995 by Arthur Sze. Reprinted with permission from Copper Canyon Press, P.O. Box 271, Port Townsend, WA 98368-0271.

Sze, Arthur. "The Leaves of a Dream Are the Leaves of an Onion." In *River River*. Lost Roads Publishers, no. 31. Providence, R.I.: Lost Roads Publishers, 1987, 13–18. Copyright © 1987 by Arthur Sze. Reprinted with permission from the author and Lost Roads Publishers.

Updike, John. "Cosmic Gall." In *Telephone Poles and Other Poems*. New York: Alfred A. Knopf, 1963, 5. Copyright © 1963 by John Updike. Reprinted with permission from Alfred A. Knopf, Inc.

Vando, Gloria. "HE 2-104: A True Planetary Nebula in the Making." In *Promesas: Geography of the Impossible*. Houston: Arte Público Press, 1993, 85. Copyright © 1993 by Gloria Vando. Reprinted with permission from Arte Público Press/University of Houston.

Van Doren, Mark. "The God of Galaxies." In *Collected and New Poems 1924–1963*. New York: Hill and Wang, 1963, 437–38. Copyright © 1963 by Mark Van Doren, renewed 1991 by Dorothy G. Van Doren. Reprinted with permission from Hill and Wang, a division of Farrar, Straus and Giroux, Inc. and Charles Van Doren.

Wallace, Ronald. "Chaos Theory." *Ploughshares* (winter 1995–1996). Copyright © 1995 by Ronald Wallace. Reprinted with permission from the author.

Webb, Charles Harper. "Heat Death." In *Reading the Water*. Boston: Northeastern University Press, 1997, 77. Copyright © 1997 by Charles Harper Webb. Reprinted with permission from Northeastern University Press.

Webb, Charles Harper. "Persistence of Sound," "Liver," and "Descent." Copyright © 1998 by Charles Harper Webb. Printed with permission from the author.

Williams, M. L. "The Uncertainty Principal." Copyright © 1998 by M. L. Williams. Printed with permission from the author.

Witte, John. "Robert Oppenheimer, 1945." Copyright © 1998 by John Witte. Printed with permission from the author.

Zimmer, Paul. "Notes Toward a Biography of Christiaan Radius, Near-Sighted Astronomer." In *The Ribs of Death*. New York: October House, 1967, 59–60. Copyright © 1967 by Paul Zimmer. Reprinted with permission from the author.

KURT BROWN is the founder of the Aspen Writers' Conference and Writers' Conferences and Festivals (a national association of directors). His poems have appeared in many periodicals, including *Crazyhorse,* the *Ontario Review,* the *Berkeley Poetry Review,* the *Southern Poetry Review,* the *Massachusetts Review,* and the *Indiana Review.* He is the editor of three annuals, *The True Subject* (Graywolf Press, 1993), *Writing It Down for James* (Beacon Press, 1995), and *Facing the Lion* (Beacon Press, 1996), which gather outstanding lectures from writers' conferences and festivals as part of the Writers on Life and Craft series. He is also the editor of *Drive, They Said: Poems about Americans and Their Cars* and coeditor with his wife, Laure-Anne Bosselaar, of *Night Out: Poems about Hotels, Motels, Restaurants, and Bars.* His first collection of poems, *Return of the Prodigals,* will be published by Four Way Books in 1999.

Index of Authors

Interior design by Will Powers
Typeset in Charlotte
by Stanton Publication Services, Inc.
Printed on acid-free 55 # Sebago Antique Cream paper
by Maple-Vail Book Manufacturing

More poetry anthologies from Milkweed Editions

Clay and Star:
Contemporary Bulgarian Poets
Translated and edited
by Lisa Sapinkopf and Georgi Belev

Drive, They Said:
Poems about Americans and Their Cars
Edited by Kurt Brown

Looking for Home:
Women Writing about Exile
Edited by Deborah Keenan and Roseann Lloyd

Minnesota Writes:
Poetry
Edited by Jim Moore and Cary Waterman

Mixed Voices:
Contemporary Poems about Music
Edited by Emilie Buchwald and Ruth Roston

Mouth to Mouth:
Poems by Twelve Contemporary Mexican Women
Edited by Forrest Gander

Night Out:
Poems about Hotels, Motels, Restaurants, and Bars
Edited by Kurt Brown and Laure-Anne Bosselaar

Passages North Anthology:
A Decade of Good Writing
Edited by Elinor Benedict

The Poet Dreaming in the Artist's House:
Contemporary Poems about the Visual Arts
Edited by Emilie Buchwald and Ruth Roston

This Sporting Life:
Contemporary American Poems
about Sports and Games
Edited by Emilie Buchwald and Ruth Roston

White Flash/Black Rain:
Women of Japan Relive the Bomb
Edited and translated by Lequita Vance-Watkins
and Aratani Mariko

Milkweed Editions publishes with the intention of making a humane impact on society, in the belief that literature is a transformative art uniquely able to convey the essential experiences of the human heart and spirit.

To that end, Milkweed publishes distinctive voices of literary merit in handsomely designed, visually dynamic books, exploring the ethical, cultural, and esthetic issues that free societies need continually to address.

Milkweed Editions is a not-for-profit press.